Epilepsy

Titles in the Diseases and Disorders series include:

DISEASES & DISORDERS

Epilepsy

Terri Dougherty

LUCENT BOOKS
A part of Gale, Cengage Learning

GALE
CENGAGE Learning

Detroit • New York • San Francisco • New Haven, Conn. • Waterville, Maine • London

GALE
CENGAGE Learning

LIBRARY OF CONGRESS CATALOGING-IN-PUBLICATION DATA

Dougherty, Terri.
  Epilepsy / by Terri Dougherty.
    p. cm. -- (Diseases & disorders)
  Includes bibliographical references and index.
  ISBN 978-1-4205-0218-3 (hardcover)
  1. Epilepsy--Juvenile literature. I. Title.
  RC372.2D68 2010
  616.8'53--dc22

                                                    2009033344

Lucent Books
27500 Drake Rd.
Farmington Hills, MI 48331

ISBN-13: 978-1-4205-0218-3
ISBN-10: 1-4205-0218-2

Printed in the United States of America
1 2 3 4 5 6 7 13 12 11 10 09

Printed by Bang Printing, Brainerd, MN, 1st Ptg., 11/2009

Table of Contents

"The Most Difficult Puzzles Ever Devised"

Charles Best, one of the pioneers in the search for a cure for diabetes, once explained what it is about medical research that intrigued him so. "It's not just the gratification of knowing one is helping people," he confided, "although that probably is a more heroic and selfless motivation. Those feelings may enter in, but truly, what I find best is the feeling of going toe to toe with nature, of trying to solve the most difficult puzzles ever devised. The answers are there somewhere, those keys that will solve the puzzle and make the patient well. But how will those keys be found?"

Since the dawn of civilization, nothing has so puzzled people—and often frightened them, as well—as the onset of illness in a body or mind that had seemed healthy before. A seizure, the inability of a heart to pump, the sudden deterioration of muscle tone in a small child—being unable to reverse such conditions or even to understand why they occur was unspeakably frustrating to healers. Even before there were names for such conditions, even before they were understood at all, each was a reminder of how complex the human body was, and how vulnerable.

While our grappling with understanding diseases has been frustrating at times, it has also provided some of humankind's most heroic accomplishments. Alexander Fleming's accidental discovery in 1928 of a mold that could be turned into penicillin has resulted in the saving of untold millions of lives. The isolation of the enzyme insulin has reversed what was once a death sentence for anyone with diabetes. There have been great strides in combating conditions for which there is not yet a cure, too. Medicines can help AIDS patients live longer, diagnostic tools such as mammography and ultrasounds can help doctors find tumors while they are treatable, and laser surgery techniques have made the most intricate, minute operations routine.

This "toe-to-toe" competition with diseases and disorders is even more remarkable when seen in a historical continuum. An astonishing amount of progress has been made in a very short time. Just two hundred years ago, the existence of germs as a cause of some diseases was unknown. In fact, it was less than 150 years ago that a British surgeon named Joseph Lister had difficulty persuading his fellow doctors that washing their hands before delivering a baby might increase the chances of a healthy delivery (especially if they had just attended to a diseased patient)!

Each book in Lucent's Diseases and Disorders series explores a disease or disorder and the knowledge that has been accumulated (or discarded) by doctors through the years. Each book also examines the tools used for pinpointing a diagnosis, as well as the various means that are used to treat or cure a disease. Finally, new ideas are presented—techniques or medicines that may be on the horizon.

Frustration and disappointment are still part of medicine, for not every disease or condition can be cured or prevented. But the limitations of knowledge are being pushed outward constantly; the "most difficult puzzles ever devised" are finding challengers every day.

Brain Storm

For Alex, the worst part is the uncertainty. He does not know when he will begin to stare and then have his arms and legs start to jerk uncontrollably. For Becca, it is the embarrassment. She will suddenly begin looking into space for moments at a time, not realizing what is going on until she comes to and sees her friends waving at her and trying to get her attention. Heather simply wants to get a good night's sleep. Some mornings she wakes up exhausted. Her night has been filled with seizures that her medication has not been able to control.

A Puzzle

Alex, Becca, and Heather have epilepsy, a mysterious condition that originates in the brain. A person with epilepsy has numerous seizures, but the cause of these seizures is often unknown. During epileptic seizures, the normal electrical activity in the brain is briefly disrupted. A sudden surge of electrical activity occurs that can impact a person's senses and actions, making a person spasm, stare, or lose consciousness. Sanjay Singh, the director of the Nebraska Epilepsy Center in Omaha, describes it this way: "Brain cells talk to one another by electrical discharges. When you have an abnormal electrical discharge in the brain which causes changes in behavior, that's a seizure. It's like an electrical storm in your brain."[1]

The seizures that result from this "electrical storm" have been baffling people for thousands of years. The word *epilepsy* comes from the Latin word *epilepsia*, meaning "to take hold of." During a seizure, an unknown force seems to take hold of a person's body, and at one time people blamed these seizures on demonic possession. Although the Greek physician Hippocrates theorized in 400 B.C. that the seizures had a natural cause, the idea persisted that they came from a curse or psychotic disorder.

The "electrical storm in the brain" caused by epilepsy is shown here in conceptual art of a brain in epileptic seizure.

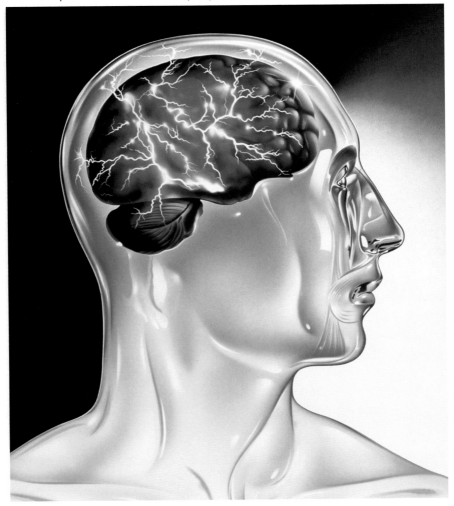

A Challenging Condition

Although cases of epilepsy have been recorded for centuries and are known to result from a physical cause, many people still do not understand the disorder. "It is still oftentimes surrounded by fear and mystery,"[2] says Eric Hargis, president and chief executive officer of the Epilepsy Foundation. A 2001 survey of American teens by the Epilepsy Foundation found that they did not see having epilepsy as a stigma; but at the same time, they did not know what it was. Almost half thought it might be a mental illness, and half thought it was contagious. Almost two-thirds would not date someone with epilepsy.

Although medical research has determined that epilepsy is caused by misfiring neurons in the brain and is not a mental illness or contagious, misperceptions about epilepsy persist. People with this seizure disorder may be labeled as *epileptics*, when the preferred term is *people with epilepsy*. Some people mistakenly think people with epilepsy are cognitively challenged, but most people with the disorder have normal intelligence. Still others think epilepsy is untreatable. Many do not realize that it is not always a lifelong illness, and that there are medications and other treatments that can control seizures.

The lack of knowledge about epilepsy by the general public is only one challenge faced by people with epilepsy, however. The condition continues to pose physical challenges as a person with epilepsy faces the possibility of a life disrupted by seizures that may not be controllable. Much progress has been made, and the majority of people with epilepsy can have their seizures controlled by medication, surgery, or other means. Yet many people with epilepsy are still seeking freedom from seizures or the frustrating side effects of their medication. Some answers have been found, but there is still much to learn about the brain and what happens when its electrical connections misfire.

CHAPTER ONE

Epilepsy and Seizures

Heather Good does not know when a seizure is happening, but she can tell when she has had one. While she is sleeping, sometimes several times a night, her muscles stiffen. Then her body begins to shake. This lasts for about a minute, but usually Good does not even wake up. In the morning she feels groggy and knows that during the night she had one or more seizures.

Good is one of 3 million people in the United States who have epilepsy. The seizure disorder can cause people to lose consciousness, collapse and jerk, or lose awareness and just stare. Each year 200,000 more people learn that they have the condition. It is found in all countries and affects people of all ages and ethnic groups. Worldwide, 50 million people have epilepsy.

Although it impacts people around the world, many people do not realize that epilepsy is a common disorder. The number of people with epilepsy is more than the combined number of people who have multiple sclerosis, cerebral palsy, muscular dystrophy, and Parkinson's disease. It is estimated that between 1 and 3 percent of people develop some type of epilepsy before they are seventy-five years old, and the Epilepsy Therapy Project estimates that up to 5 percent of people worldwide will have a seizure at some point in their lives.

Nonetheless, epilepsy is often misunderstood. The seizures that people with epilepsy experience can be frightening and unpredictable. "Epilepsy has afflicted human beings since the dawn of our species and has been recognized since the earliest medical writings," notes Steven Schachter, a professor of neurology at Harvard Medical School. "In fact, few medical conditions have attracted so much attention and generated so much controversy as epilepsy."[3]

Paramedics tend to a woman having an epileptic episode. Seizures can cause people to lose consciousness and collapse and jerk uncontrollably.

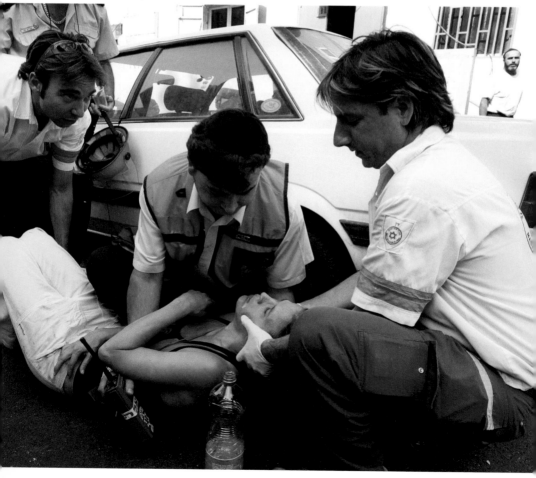

Brain Damage and Seizures

Epilepsy is the result of something going wrong inside the brain, but the seizures themselves do not usually cause long-term problems with a person's intellect or reasoning, says Roy Sucholeiki of Central DuPage Hospital in Chicago. Although having a seizure is not good for the brain, an occasional seizure will not damage it. "There are brilliant people who have epilepsy," Sucholeiki notes. "It is not completely controlled, and they [do] not seem to have the loss of intellectual abilities over time."

Epilepsy seldom causes brain damage, although a severe, prolonged seizure could cause some cognitive delay. Certain types of epilepsy are more likely to cause brain damage, notes William Davis Gaillard, the division chief of epilepsy and neurophysiology at Children's National Medical Center in Washington, D.C.

If cognitive delay is noted, it may be unclear whether the epilepsy caused the problem or whether there is another, underlying problem causing both the epilepsy and other problems. "It's the chicken or the egg," Sucholeiki says. "If you have epilepsy that's that bad, there must be some underlying abnormality that's there to begin with that might cause [impairment]."

Roy Sucholeiki, telephone interview with author, May 11, 2009.

William Davis Gaillard, telephone interview with author, June 12, 2009.

Part of what makes epilepsy so difficult to understand is that its seizures may come at any time, without warning. A person does not experience the symptoms of epilepsy constantly. A person may be seizure-free for days or longer and then have another episode that involves staring or convulsions. The unpredictability of the condition, and the unusual nature of some seizures, make epilepsy challenging to live with and to treat.

What Is Epilepsy?

Many questions surround epilepsy, but it is clear that this chronic seizure disorder is rooted in the brain. A person is considered to have epilepsy after having two or more seizures that are not caused by another medical condition. When a person has a seizure, something happens in the brain that impacts the nervous system, causing it to go haywire. When things go wrong inside the brain, it can affect the way a person's body moves or his or her awareness of what is going on around him or her.

A seizure is commonly thought of as a jerking movement, but many different types of seizures exist. A person may stare and be unaware of what is happening or may become confused about his or her whereabouts. A person may lose consciousness for only a few seconds or a fraction of a second. Lip smacking, sudden jerks, a bicycling movement of the legs, picking at clothes or the air, as well as shaking movements, all can be signs that something is going wrong inside the brain and is causing a person to have a seizure.

Epilepsy itself is not an illness; rather, it is a term that indicates that a person has recurring seizures. "Epilepsy is not a disease, it's a symptom," explains Roy Sucholeiki of Central DuPage Hospital in Chicago. "Epilepsy by definition only means that the brain of the person has a tendency to seize, to the extent treatment is indicated. It's kind of like looking at a fever, which can be caused by many kinds of infections. Fever is not a disease, it's a symptom."[4]

Diagnosing Epilepsy

A person with epilepsy has recurring seizures that are rooted in an underlying problem in the brain. Before diagnosing a person with epilepsy, a doctor will determine whether a person is having seizures and then look for a way to explain why the seizures are happening. A person may experience shaking of the body that is not a seizure, so the doctor will ask about how the seizures occur and what they are like. When a person is falling asleep, for example, the body may jerk slightly. This common occurrence is not a seizure.

A doctor will also ask if the seizures are a recurring problem. People with epilepsy have more than one seizure, and often they have many of them. A person may have only one seizure but not have epilepsy. A single seizure could be caused by a stroke, infection, or brain injury, among other things. If a person does not have more than one seizure, he or she does not have epilepsy. However, if a person has more seizures after having a brain injury, stroke, or infection or often for an unknown reason, that person is considered to have epilepsy. The key is whether the seizure is a one-time event.

Some nonepileptic medical conditions also cause seizures, so a doctor attempting a diagnosis of epilepsy must perform medical tests to determine if a seizure may have been caused by another illness. For example, a fainting spell may cause a person to lose consciousness, and even jerk or shake, but it is caused by a

A technician administers an EEG test to a young boy. The test will reveal the structure of the patient's brain and help make a diagnosis of epilepsy.

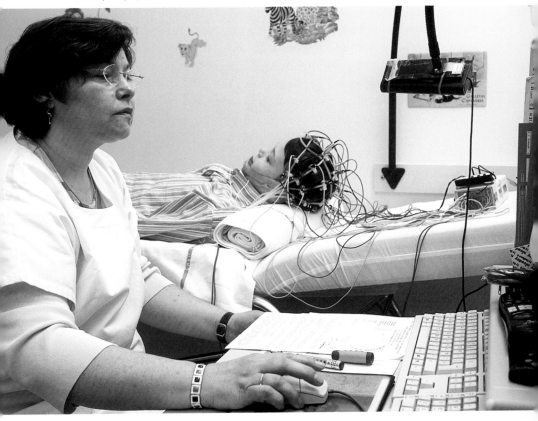

drop in blood flow to the brain rather than a problem that originates in the brain. A person whose salt levels in the bloodstream fall too low, perhaps due to rigorous exercise or an illness that produces diarrhea or vomiting, may have a seizure. A glucose imbalance in the body, associated with diabetes, can produce a seizure, and a panic attack or sleep disorder may also be mistaken for epilepsy. Kidney problems and liver failure can also result in seizures. These seizures disrupt the way the body is functioning, but are not caused by a problem with the brain's electrical activity..

To make a diagnosis of epilepsy, a doctor will use information gathered from a number of sources. Blood tests can determine if the seizures have an environmental cause, such as exposure to lead, certain chemicals, street drugs, or alcohol. Other tests examine a person's reflexes and coordination as well as mental functions such as senses and memory. A person will also have an electroencephalograph (EEG) so the doctor can look at brain waves, and brain-imaging tests will allow the doctor to look at the structure of the patient's brain. Certain brain wave patterns may lead to a diagnosis of epilepsy, and the doctor will take them into account as well as the conditions surrounding a seizure and a patient's medical history when making a diagnosis of epilepsy.

How Does the Brain Work?

It is important for doctors to look at brain waves and an image of a person's brain when making a diagnosis because they provide important clues about how the brain is functioning. Seizures begin in the brain, and looking at how a person's brain works is part of the solution to unraveling the mystery of epilepsy.

The brain is a complicated organ, with billions of nerve cells sending messages through the body to control everything a person does, from breathing to blinking, speaking, thinking, and moving. A person's conscious brain is a complex place, as the cells work together to make the body function. As the control center for the nervous system, the brain absorbs information from the senses and reacts in a fraction of a second, enabling a person to see, hear, reason, and interact with others. Nerve cells provide the thoughts and reasoning that allow one to read a book or do a math problem and have the coordination needed to hit a home run or ride a bike.

The brain contains 50 to 100 billion nerve cells, called neurons. At one end of each microscopic neuron are dendrites, which look like branches and reach out to gather information in the area around the cell. The dendrites are connected to the cell body. At the other end of the nerve cell is a long, thin tail called the axon, which takes the neuron's information and passes it to other nerve cells.

A network of nerve cells in the body allows information to travel to and from the brain. To rapidly carry information from one nerve cell to another, the body uses electricity, with each nerve cell acting like a battery with electrical properties. There are gaps called synapses between the nerve cells; to send information over this gap, the nerve cells fire messages using an electrical signal. A chemical called a neurotransmitter carries this signal from one neuron to another. The message a neuron sends can quiet or excite the neuron with which it is communicating, so it gets ready to rest or fire a message itself. This method of relaying information between neurons allows information to travel in a split second, letting the body quickly react to all that is going on around it.

To efficiently process all the information coming at it every second and distribute the necessary actions, the brain uses neural pathways. Inside the brain, the neurons are not just gathering and sending information to and from a few cells but are communicating with each other over a complex web of connections. "Each nerve cell is capable of thousands of connections with its neighbors," Sucholeiki says. "The number of connections is on the order of trillions. It's been said that there are more connections in the brain than stars in the galaxy. All these connections and networks have to have nicely balanced chemical and electrical properties."[5]

Problems occur when something disturbs this balance between the electrical and chemical properties in the brain. A tumor, stroke, something that develops at birth, or a certain drug exposure might compromise the balance between neurons. When this happens, the brain could go into a seizure.

Every day, every minute, every second, the brain's neurons are at work, firing electrical impulses as they communicate with each other. Given the complicated nature of the brain's operations, it is not that seizures occur that surprises Sucholeiki but that they do not occur more often. "By the very nature of our brain, the chance of having a seizure is not 0, it's about 9 percent," he says. "It's not necessarily surprising that the brain is capable of seizing, what's interesting is what do people, even those with epilepsy, do to keep it from seizing? Even when we sleep the brain is always turned on. It is primed for excitation."[6]

A Breakdown in the Brain

As it gathers and sends information, the brain is not operating in an orderly fashion. When it is working as it should, the brain's electrical discharges are complex and disordered. Neurons are communicating with each other in a complicated way that follows no set pattern. Writers Jerry Adler and Eliza Gray describe it this way: "A normal brain is governed by chaos; neurons fire unpredictably, following laws no computer, let alone neurologist, could hope to understand, even if they can recognize it on an EEG. It is what we call consciousness, perhaps the most mathematically complex phenomenon in the universe."[7]

In this illustration a neurotransmitter (in blue) transmits across the gap in a synapse to send electrical information to the brain.

Misfiring neurons can cause a person with epilepsy to have staring spells that last from a few seconds to 10 minutes.

This natural disorder comes to a halt when a person has a seizure. The normal electrical discharges in the brain become disrupted, and the brain's neurons begin firing at the same time. This may occur all over the brain at once, happen only in one area of the brain, or start in one area and spread to the rest of the brain. When the neurons start firing simultaneously, or too many neurons in one area fire at once, the body experiences a seizure. The delicate balance in the brain that has neurons sending and receiving information designed to quiet or excite other neurons becomes unhinged. "There is a fine balance in the brain between factors that begin electrical activity and factors that restrict it, and there are also systems that limit the spread of electrical activity," Schachter explains. "During a seizure, these limits break down, and abnormal electrical discharges can occur and spread to whole groups of neighboring cells at once."[8]

The Dangers of Epilepsy

The impact of a seizure can vary depending on how much of the brain is impacted by the seizure and which areas of the brain are affected. The misfiring neurons may cause a person to have a staring spell lasting a few seconds or may make a person jerk uncontrollably for ten minutes. Although they have different physical manifestations, any uncontrolled seizure is a serious event that poses a threat to the person with epilepsy.

In some cases, epilepsy can be fatal. It has been estimated that up to 50,000 people in the United States die each year from seizures and causes related to them. A person having a seizure may be injured by falling to the floor or even by drowning in a bathtub filled with only a few inches of water. Likewise, a person who has uncontrolled seizures cannot drive a car because of the danger of losing consciousness.

Although it is not common, a seizure itself can cause death. A long seizure, called a tonic-colonic status epilepticus, which lasts thirty minutes, can cause brain damage or be fatal. About 15 percent of people with epilepsy experience status epilepticus, according to the Epilepsy Foundation. Choking on vomit is another danger. In a small number of cases, a person vomits while having a seizure; if the vomit does not drain properly from his or her mouth, the person could choke.

People with epilepsy may also die in their sleep. This is called sudden unexplained death in epilepsy (SUDEP). The risk of this happening is about one in three thousand each year for people with epilepsy. "No one is sure about the cause of death in SUDEP. Some researchers think that a seizure causes an irregular heart rhythm. More recent studies have suggested that the person may suffocate from impaired breathing, fluid in the lungs, and being face down on the bedding,"[9] Schachter notes.

The Implications of Epilepsy

The risk of death is very real for people with epilepsy, and the condition also brings challenges to their lives every single day. People with epilepsy must learn to cope with the unpredictable seizures that can impact what they can and cannot do. Adults are not allowed to drive a car for a number of months after having a seizure, limiting their mobility and independence. A person's career choices can be impacted by the possibility that he or she may suffer a seizure. In addition, social implications and misunderstandings abound about epilepsy. "Part of the problem with it is not so much that it's not well known, but that it's extremely stigmatizing," Sucholeiki says. "It's somewhat taboo for a family to talk about it; there is a lot of shame. That creates an almost unique social problem associated with the medical problem."[10]

People with epilepsy often face unnecessary hurdles because most people know so little about the condition. Although epilepsy is not contagious, sometimes a parent is unnecessarily concerned that one child will get it from another. "Most people don't think that way, but it's common enough that I need to explain it to the average patient who comes in so that [misunderstanding] is cleared up,"[11] Sucholeiki says.

People with epilepsy also must deal with ignorance about the disorder when they look for a job. The unemployment rate for employable people with epilepsy is much higher than the national average. Eric Hargis, the president and chief executive

Fighting for Respect

People with epilepsy come from all walks of life, from children in grade school to scientists, firefighters, and teachers. However, its impact is often underestimated, and the condition is not something that is often discussed. At one time, people with epilepsy were prohibited from marrying or having children. In the past, people have tried to hide the disease because of its stigma and the misunderstandings about the disorder.

"People have not been willing to talk about epilepsy. I think there's a historic stigma which goes back to the perhaps under-standable reactions people historically had to seeing someone experience a seizure," notes Warren Lammert, cofounder and chairman of the Epilepsy Therapy Project.

Epilepsy has been thought to be both a sign that someone was divine or godlike and a sign that a person was a witch or possessed by the devil. "It was not understood until recent centuries that a seizure is just excessive electrical activity in the brain," Lammert notes.

Quoted in National Public Radio, "Living with the Uncertainty of Epilepsy," April 28, 2009. www.npr.org/templates/story/story.php?storyId =103577442.

This nineteenth-century engraving reinforces the outdated idea that people with epilepsy were bewitched or possessed by the devil.

officer of the Epilepsy Foundation, sees a lack of understanding about epilepsy contributing to this rate. "If they're not aware of what the ramifications of epilepsy actually are, they are going to be very inclined not to hire people,"[12] he says.

In some cultures, religious views about epilepsy stigmatize people with the disorder. Former California congressman Tony Coelho's parents, who were Portuguese immigrants, could not accept the fact that their son had epilepsy when he was diagnosed as a teen. They believed that epilepsy was the result of possession by the devil. Coelho wanted to become a priest, but he was denied admission to the Jesuit seminary because of his epilepsy. He was also refused admission into the Army. He later served in Congress and became chairman of the Epilepsy Foundation board, where he worked to break down the stigma carried by epilepsy. He drew on his experiences as he worked to get legislation passed that prohibited discrimination against people with disabilities. "What I once considered a curse forced me to face life, shaped me and strengthened me," he says. "Above all, it gave me a mission for people with disabilities."[13]

The Epilepsy Foundation is working to remove the stigma from the disorder. Part of the misunderstanding may stem from a desire of families to try to keep the condition a secret. "Epilepsy is often kept in the shadows," Hargis says. "We have parents who are stigma coaches, who tell their children, 'Don't let anyone at school know.' You don't have parents of children

Reducing the risk of SUDEP

To reduce the risk of sudden unexplained death in epilepsy syndrome, or SUDEP, the Epilepsy Therapy Project recommends:

- Taking all seizure medication regularly, as prescribed.
- Avoiding heavy alcohol use and recreational drugs.
- Getting regular sleep and avoiding fatigue.

Steven Schachter, "How Serious Are Seizures?" *Epilepsy.com.* www.epilepsy.com/101/ep101_death.

with asthma or diabetes tell[ing] children that." Offering information about the facts about epilepsy can help that stigma dis-
appear, he notes, and help people understand the seizure
disorder rather than fear it. "There is a whole impact on quality
of life you don't necessarily see with other chronic conditions,"
Hargis says. "The goal here is to have epilepsy recognized as a
medical condition that for most people is treatable."[14]

CHAPTER TWO

Seizures and Their Causes

To improve the quality of life for people with epilepsy and to find the right treatment, doctors do their best to find out what is causing a person's seizures. Although the cause is often not found, a person can still be treated for seizures. Therefore, doctors try to gather as much information as possible about what is impacting the brain in order to determine how best to treat the patient.

Finding the cause of a person's epilepsy is not a simple matter. The brain is a complex organ, and there are a number of factors that can cause a person to have seizures. There may be a physical cause or a genetic one, or the cause may be unclear. Sometimes doctors can determine why a person has seizures, but most of the time the cause remains a mystery.

An Array of Causes

In about half of the cases, epilepsy begins before a person is twenty-five years old. This is because the brain is more susceptible to seizures when it is immature. There are a number of things that can impact a child's brain and bring on seizures.

Sometimes an abnormality in the brain is present at birth that leads to epilepsy. The disorder also may be caused by a lack of oxygen at birth, a head injury that brings on scarring, or

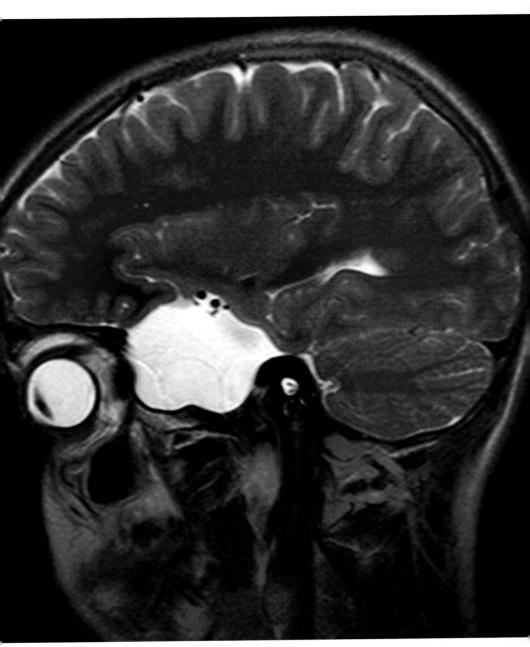

An abnormal collection of spinal fluid in the cranial fossa of the brain is shown in blue. Though benign, it can sometimes cause seizures that imitate epileptic symptoms.

an illness. There may be physical causes relating to epilepsy, such as too much spinal fluid, a tumor, or a tangle of blood vessels in the brain.

Epilepsy is sometimes linked to other conditions. In children, epilepsy can be associated with autism, developmental delays, or cerebral palsy, notes Roy Sucholeiki of Chicago's Central DuPage Hospital. A baby who is small for his or her age or one who has a seizure within the first month of life is also at risk for developing epilepsy. "Anything that affects the brain may put it also at risk for development of a seizure problem,"[15] Sucholeiki says.

Sometimes children have seizures when they are young but outgrow them and do not have epilepsy as adults. About 2 to 5 percent of babies and children under age five are prone to having seizures when they have a high fever. Most of these children outgrow this tendency.

Children often outgrow certain types of epilepsy as well. About 15 percent of children with epilepsy have a syndrome called benign rolandic epilepsy. Children with this type of epilepsy usually start having seizures between ages six and eight and usually stop having them by they time they are fifteen. Children with a type of epilepsy called childhood absence epilepsy also usually outgrow their seizures. About 2 to 8 percent of children with epilepsy have this type of disorder, which usually begins between ages four and eight and is eventually outgrown.

Benign rolandic epilepsy and childhood absence epilepsy usually have a genetic cause, and children inherit their predisposition to epilepsy from their parents. Just as the way people look is a result of the combined genes they inherit from their parents, the way the cells in their brain are structured is also inherited. If a person inherits the brain-cell structure related to epilepsy, he or she will have a greater likelihood of developing the disorder. A person who has a brother, sister, or parent with epilepsy has about a 4 to 8 percent chance of developing epilepsy.

If a person develops epilepsy as a young adult, a head injury is the most common cause. Although not everyone who has a head injury has recurring seizures, some people do. A car accident or a serious fall may result in a head injury that leads to

Epilepsy is often linked to other disorders such as autism in children and Alzheimer's disease in older adults.

epilepsy. A person in the military may begin having seizures after receiving a head injury from a bomb blast. Whether a person will get seizures after a head injury depends on what part of the head was injured, what caused the injury, and whether the person is genetically predisposed to developing epilepsy.

People in middle age who develop epilepsy may have seizures because of a head injury, stroke, or brain tumor. In people over age sixty-five, a degenerative condition such as Alzheimer's disease or a stroke are the most common causes of epilepsy.

Although epilepsy has many causes, in a great number of cases the reason for a person's repeated seizures is never found. Certain risk factors—such as a head injury, an infection, or having family members with epilepsy—make a person more susceptible to epilepsy; however, many people with the disorder do not have these risk factors. The Epilepsy Foundation estimates that no cause for a person's seizures can be found in seven out of ten people with epilepsy. "Often we just don't know how epilepsy gets started,"[16] admits Steven Schachter, a professor of neurology at Harvard Medical School.

A Variety of Symptoms

Because the brain's wiring is so complex, seizures can produce a number of symptoms. In one person a seizure can result in convulsive jerking, but another person may experience mental confusion. A person having a seizure may also simply stare, smack his or her lips, or move a hand uncontrollably.

Seizures also vary by intensity and duration, with some people experiencing mild symptoms for short amounts of time and others having longer, more violent seizures. The seizures may be so mild that they are not noticed or so severe that they put someone's life in danger.

Seizure Location

One factor that has a large impact on what happens to a person during a seizure is where the seizure occurs in the brain. Different areas of the brain control different functions in the body, so the way a person acts during a seizure will depend on which areas are impacted by the misfiring neurons.

The temporal lobes on the side of the head are associated with emotion and memory. A person's ability to understand language is also in this region of the brain. A person with temporal lobe epilepsy may have seizures that begin with unusual feelings or emotions and may include the sense that even familiar people or places are strange. It may involve hearing voices that are not there or a strange taste or smell. People with temporal lobe epilepsy may not understand what other people are saying, may become unresponsive, or may make unusual movements, such as smacking the lips or rubbing their hands together repetitively. Often, the seizures spread to another part of the brain and bring on convulsions.

The frontal lobe controls personality, anxiety, alertness, and behavior as well as a person's ability to speak, plan, and organize. The motor cortex area of the frontal lobe controls movement. A person may experience jerking of the thumb, for example, if the part of the brain that controls movement in that area is affected by a seizure. If the muscles that control speech are affected, a person will be unable to talk. Frontal lobe seizures may also involve having the head jerk to one side, screaming, laughing, running, a bicycling movement of the legs, or having the arm rise. A seizure that begins in the frontal lobe may spread and bring on convulsions, jerking, and stiffness.

A seizure may also begin in the occipital lobe in the back of the brain, which controls vision. A person who has a seizure that starts in the back of the brain may see images that are not really there. Seizures may also begin in the parietal lobe, which is in the center of the brain, although it is not common for seizures to begin in this area. The parietal lobe controls sensation, and a seizure that begins here may involve tingling or numbness.

Although each area of the brain controls a specific function and seizures in the different areas produce different symptoms, they do have something in common. "The underlying common thread is a disturbance in the electrical and chemical properties of the brain," Sucholeiki says. "It's an abnormal and spontaneous activation of some part of the brain so you get an involuntary experience. If it's intense enough you lose consciousness of what's happening to you momentarily."[17]

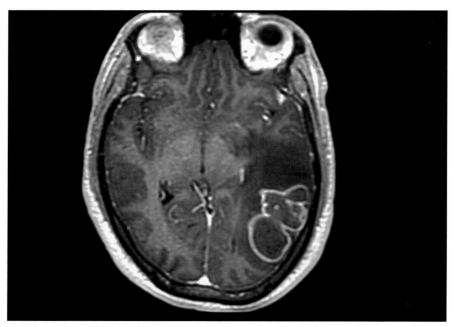

This MRI shows a cerebral abscess (in red) located in the temporal occipital region of the brain. The abscess is responsible for epileptic seizures.

Here, There, or Everywhere

When a person has a seizure, neurons start firing at the same time. This may happen in only one area of the brain, or it may start everywhere in the brain at the same time. In general, seizures are broken into two categories: generalized seizures and partial seizures.

When a seizure begins in one area of the brain, it is called a partial seizure. A person's body may stiffen, or he or she may feel strange. A partial seizure's impact on a person's body depends on where in the brain the abnormal electrical discharge occurs.

When a seizure happens over the entire brain at the same time and impacts both sides of the brain, it is called a primary generalized seizure. During a primary generalized seizure, a person may experience symptoms such as stiffness, jerking, and loss of consciousness that are caused by misfiring neurons impacting the entire brain. "With a generalized seizure, the electrical storm effects go through the hemispheres simultaneously,"[18] explains Sanjay Singh, director of the Nebraska Epilepsy Center in Omaha.

The Types of Generalized Seizures

When a person mentions the word *epilepsy* or *seizure*, a vision of a person having a tonic-clonic seizure usually comes to mind. This type of primary generalized seizure, formerly called

Music and Seizures

It is very rare, but sometimes a person's seizures will be triggered by a song or style of music. Stacey Gayle was twenty-one when she had two major absence seizures and was diagnosed with epilepsy. "I didn't convulse; instead I'd basically fall asleep," she says. "Strangers thought I was either drunk or crazy."

She eventually realized that she got seizures when she heard the song "Temperature" by Sean Paul. She shared her story with *Cosmopolitan* magazine, relating, "In 2006, I was at a barbecue when my friend asked if I'd heard Sean Paul's new song 'Temperature.' Seconds after she hit play, I seized. Several weeks later, I almost fell overboard on a boat because I seized as the same song came on."

Gayle says that several types of music would cause her to have seizures. A diseased area in the right temporal lobe area of her brain was misfiring and causing the seizures. She went through testing to determine the location of the seizures and had an operation to remove the diseased area.

The operation was successful, and Gayle is seizure free. She plans to become a teacher and is thankful for the freedom the successful operation has given her. "I'm so thankful for all the parts of everyday life that I get to experience again."

Quoted in Melissa Daly, "Hearing Music Gave Me Seizures," *Cosmopolitan*, August 2008, p. 154.

a grand mal seizure, impacts the entire brain. It may begin with a grunt or a scream, which happens because the respiratory muscles contract involuntarily. A person loses consciousness, and the body becomes stiff because it is gripped by a muscular contraction. A person may turn pale or blue, as breathing is temporarily stopped. After a person goes through the tonic—or stiff—phase, which lasts for less than a minute, the clonic phase of uncontrolled jerking begins as the muscles alternately contract and react. The seizure usually lasts a few minutes.

Although a tonic-clonic seizure is one of the best-known types of seizures, a person may experience only the tonic phase. During a tonic seizure, the body's muscles tighten, causing the person to stiffen. This usually occurs when a person is sleeping, but if it occurs when he or she is standing, the person often falls down. Rarely, a person will experience a clonic seizure, which involves only the jerking movements of the arms and legs.

A person may also experience a myoclonic seizure, a generalized seizure that involves one or more brief jerks that last only about a second. A person's muscles typically contract rapidly on both sides of the body. A person's arm may fly up or foot may jerk. "Even people without epilepsy can experience myoclonus in hiccups or in a sudden jerk that may wake you up as you're just falling asleep," notes Orrin Devinsky, an epilepsy expert from New York University. "These things are normal."[19]

Whereas a person's muscles rapidly contract and relax during a myoclonic seizure, they become extremely weak during a type of generalized seizure called an atonic seizure. When a person's muscles suddenly lose strength, his or her body may sag. A person who is sitting down may fall forward, and a person who is standing during this type of seizure may be injured while falling to the floor. A person usually stays conscious during these seizures, which may also be called drop attacks or drop seizures.

Absence Seizures

Another type of generalized seizure impacts a person's consciousness more than his or her muscles. Absence seizures, a well-known and common type of generalized seizure, involve sudden, momentary memory loss. A person becomes unaware of his or her surroundings for a second or two or perhaps for half a minute.

The symptoms of an absence seizure, which is also known as a petit mal seizure, may be very mild or brief. A person may stare upward slightly for just a second. He or she may have a staggering gait. Facial muscles may twitch. A person may stare for a few seconds, not hearing anything going on around him or her, and then return to normal without realizing there had been a seizure. About 70 percent of the time, absence seizures cease by age eighteen.

Although a person typically outgrows absence seizures, they can have a significant impact on a child if they remain undiagnosed. Absence seizures can lead to misunderstandings if a teacher is unaware of a child's condition. A child who does not respond when a teacher calls his or her name may be reprimanded for not paying attention or may be accused of disobedience. He or she may also miss portions of what is being taught and may be scolded for not listening if he or she does

Because absence seizures can happen hundreds of times a day, an undiagnosed child who has epilepsy can be labeled uncooperative and disobedient.

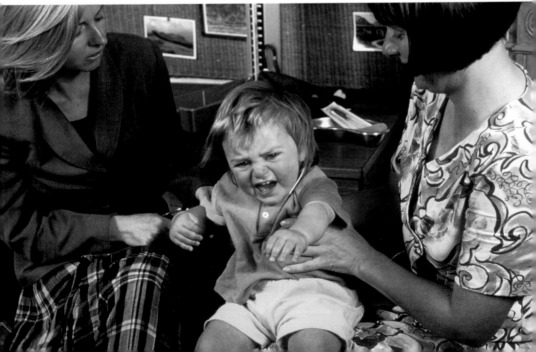

not understand the lesson. These seizures can happen hundreds of times a day, and if a child is not accurately diagnosed, he may be unfairly labeled as uncooperative. "It is important to recognize that the child is not daydreaming, and is not failing to pay attention," notes Donald Weaver, the author of *Epilepsy and Seizures: Everything You Need to Know.* "He or she is genuinely unaware."[20]

The Types of Partial Seizures

Although a person having an absence seizure is unaware of what is going on around him or her, that is not the case with all types of seizures. A person having a simple partial seizure remains conscious and aware during the entire episode.

A simple partial seizure begins in only one area of the brain. Depending on which part of the brain is affected, the seizure may involve uncontrollable twitching, hallucinations such as a ringing sound that is not there, or abnormal sensations such as a floating or spinning feeling. A person may sweat or be nauseous, have a flushed look, or feel afraid. A person may also

A Child's Brain Is a Complex Place

Over time, a person's brain learns to use certain neural pathways more frequently. A child's brain is even more complex than an adult's because it is primed to change as the child matures. "The brain is the only organ that continues to mature physically over the years," says Roy Sucholeiki of Central DuPage Hospital. "At birth it's only half to three-quarters of what it's going to be as an adult. At birth you have almost double the amount of connections among neurons in the brain you end up with as an adult. The adult brain is the pruning back of undesirable connections that are there in infancy."

Roy Sucholeiki, telephone interview with author, May 11, 2009.

have trouble understanding what others are saying or have trouble reading. The seizure usually lasts less than two minutes. "With a partial seizure, the electrical storm just involves a small part of the brain," notes Singh. "These are much more common than generalized seizures."[21]

A partial seizure may not remain limited to one area; it may spread to another area of the brain or travel throughout the brain. When a partial seizure impacts another area of the brain, it is called a complex partial seizure; when it travels throughout the brain, it is called a secondary generalized seizure.

A person having a complex partial seizure, which impacts more than one area of the brain, usually becomes unresponsive or unconscious. A person may first have an unusual feeling in the abdomen, dizziness, or smell a strange odor that is not there. As the seizure spreads, it impacts areas of the brain that make a person alert. During this part of the seizure, a person's eyes may be open. Nonetheless, he or she does not sense what is going on around him or her and may appear to be daydreaming. A person may make chewing motions or smack the lips, pick at clothing, make a bicycling motion with the legs, or behave oddly in other ways. "Less often, people may repeat words or phrases, laugh, scream, or cry. Some people do things during these seizures that can be dangerous or embarrassing, such as walking into traffic or taking their clothes off,"[22] notes Devinsky. These seizures usually last a few minutes. A person usually cannot remember the seizure afterward and may be very tired.

A partial seizure may spread to the entire brain to become a secondary generalized seizure. The seizure may begin with the twitching of a finger, an unusual feeling, or a visual hallucination, and then it spreads. When the secondary generalized seizure spreads, a person may fall down and begin to jerk and twitch.

Seizure Stages

Some seizures have a definite beginning, middle, and end. A person may sense that a seizure is approaching before his or her body begins to jerk or twitch. The sense that a seizure is about to occur is most common in people with partial complex seizures.

When a person has a warning that a seizure is imminent, it is called an aura. The aura may be a feeling of dizziness or nausea, or it may be a sense of déjà vu or a feeling of lightheadedness. The seizure then progresses to the second stage, which may include involuntary jerking, eye rolling, falling down, or convulsions.

After the second stage of the seizure, the person returns to normal. During the third stage, the brain recovers from the seizure. This may take a few seconds, minutes, or hours. A person is often very tired after a seizure and may go into a deep sleep.

Epilepsy Syndromes

People with epilepsy experience seizures in different ways, depending on which parts of the brain the seizure impacts and how it begins and spreads. Sometimes, however, the signs and symptoms they experience are common to a certain type of epilepsy. These types of epilepsy are called epilepsy syndromes. Syndromes have a number of characteristics in common, such as the type of seizure a person has, the behavior during the seizure, similar EEG patterns, and genetic factors. People with the same syndrome may be roughly the same age when seizures begin, have seizures that begin in the same part of the brain, and respond in similar ways to medications.

If a patient's epilepsy can be classified under a certain syndrome, this can help the doctor determine which medications and treatments will work best for the patient. It can also help the doctor predict whether the patient's epilepsy will go away or lessen in severity over time.

A child diagnosed with benign rolandic epilepsy, for example, can expect to one day be seizure free. This type of epilepsy generally impacts children six to eight years old and involves seizures that result in twitching or numbness of the face or tonic-clonic seizures during sleep. It is called *benign* because in almost every case children outgrow it and stop having seizures by age fifteen.

Many children diagnosed with absence epilepsy also often are seizure free by the time they are adults. With childhood absence epilepsy, seizures usually begin between the ages of four and eight. A person with childhood absence epilepsy experiences as many as fifty staring spells a day, during which they are not aware of what is going on around them for a short period of time. They may also have tonic-clonic seizures. This type of epilepsy tends to run in families and usually responds to treatment. By the time the children grow into adults, the seizures are usually gone.

A similar type of epilepsy is juvenile absence epilepsy. This type of epilepsy begins a little later in life than childhood absence epilepsy, usually between ages ten and seventeen. As with childhood absence epilepsy, a person with juvenile absence epilepsy experiences staring episodes and inattentiveness and may have tonic-clonic seizures. It also tends to run in families. Unlike people with childhood absence epilepsy, those with juvenile absence epilepsy are unlikely to outgrow the disorder and will probably have to take seizure-controlling medication for their entire lives.

A person with juvenile absence epilepsy may develop juvenile myoclonic epilepsy in late childhood or early adulthood. Juvenile myoclonic seizures involve jerks of the arms that may be followed by a tonic-clonic seizure. This type of epilepsy may be triggered by strobe lights, video games, or, occasionally, doing mathematical calculations. It can also be triggered by alcohol or a lack of sleep. It can usually be controlled with medication, but it is typically not outgrown.

Researchers study children's EEG recordings to determine what type of epileptic symptoms the child is experiencing.

Rarely, a child will develop a progressive myoclonic epilepsy syndrome, which can involve both myoclonic seizures that cause jerking movements and tonic-clonic seizures that involve convulsions. Balance problems, stiff muscles, and mental impairment are associated with this type of epilepsy, which may be caused by one of several rare genetic disorders. This type of epilepsy is very difficult to treat.

Another rare syndrome is Landau-Kleffner syndrome. It begins in children who are three to seven years old and involves speech impairment and some seizures. In children with this syndrome, speech develops normally but the child gradually loses the ability to speak. Children with this syndrome have similar EEG patterns when asleep. Medication and surgical options are available for treatment. The disorder sometimes goes away on its own, but some children have permanent language difficulties.

Sometimes seizures begin when a child is less than a year old. Young children who have febrile seizures, or seizures that occur when the child has a fever, typically outgrow them. However, children with infantile spasms, or West syndrome, often experience rapid jerking movements and have developmental delays. They may go on to have other forms of epilepsy. Some children develop Lennox-Gastaut syndrome, an uncommon type of epilepsy that is associated with mental impairment. Patients with this type of epilepsy have seizures that are difficult to control and may have personality issues. These seizures can include absence seizures, tonic seizures that cause stiffening, and atonic, or drop, seizures. Because people with this type of epilepsy may fall down unexpectedly, they may wear a helmet. Seizures usually begin when a person is between two and six years old, and people with this type of epilepsy typically need care throughout their lives. A similar but separate syndrome is ring chromosome 20 epilepsy syndrome, which is characterized by seizures that are difficult to control, subtle seizures at night, and various degrees of behavior problems. A person with this type of epilepsy may be of normal intelligence or mentally handicapped. Ring chromosome 20 is caused by a rare chromosome malformation.

Rasmussen's syndrome also has serious implications. It usually begins in children who are a little over one year old or younger than fourteen, and it involves numerous seizures and mental impairment. A person may have a weak arm or leg and may have difficulty speaking. To stop the seizures and the loss of mental function, a radical step may be taken: removal of half of the brain. The surgery is usually effective, and the patient learns to adjust, having the ability to walk, run, and usually speak even after half the brain is removed.

Brain surgery may also help children with a condition called hypothalamic hamartoma. Children with this syndrome will exhibit signs of early puberty, have partial seizures, and will become irritable between seizures. A growth of abnormal tissue is the cause of these problems, and surgery can provide relief. If surgery is not an option, medication can be used as a treatment.

Triggers

People with the same type of epilepsy syndrome may find that their seizures are set off by similar things. Although often it is not known exactly what provokes a seizure, sometimes a person realizes that a specific sound or condition will bring one on

Surgeons perform eleven-hour brain surgery on a young patient with Rasmussen's syndrome. The surgery may relieve a condition which causes epileptic seizures.

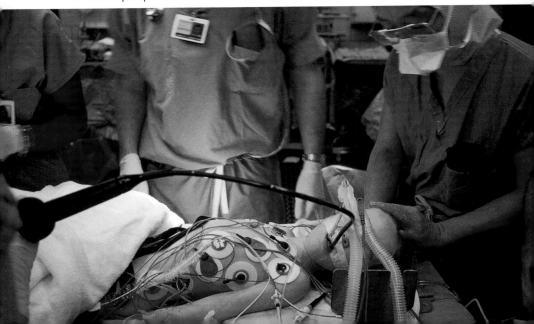

or make seizures occur more frequently. These conditions or sensations are called triggers.

People with a type of epilepsy called reflex epilepsy have seizures after being exposed to something that stimulates a seizure. This can include reading, writing, or seeing flashing lights. Even hearing church bells, seeing certain colors, or driving past a line of trees with the sun flickering through them can trigger a seizure.

People with epilepsy may also have seizures triggered by their physical condition. Lack of sleep or illness may trigger a seizure. Stress can also be a seizure trigger. For some people, simply falling asleep or waking up can bring on a seizure.

In some cases a nutritional deficiency—such as a lack of vitamins or minerals—may cause a seizure to occur. A person who misses a dose of medication or who takes an over-the-counter medication that decreases the effectiveness of

In some people with epilepsy, seizures are triggered by playing video games or watching television.

epilepsy medication may trigger a seizure. Using drugs or heavy use of alcohol can also be a seizure trigger.

In some people, seizures are triggered by things that are very subtle, perhaps even a thought. Doing arithmetic or playing video games can bring on a seizure, and some people report very odd seizure triggers, including playing mah-jongg, the voice of Mary Hart on television, or certain types of music. An episode of the television show *Pokémon* was linked to seizures in some children—thought to be brought on by quickly flashing colors in the animation—but those type of triggers are very unusual. "In the vast majority of people with epilepsy there are generally no specific triggers," Sucholeiki says. "People often report that stress will be more likely to bring one on, or perhaps sleep deprivation. In some rare cases music might provoke it, but that's more of a curiosity and very rare."[23]

The Individual Impact

Perhaps one of the most challenging facets of epilepsy is learning why some people experience very unusual seizure triggers, from a voice on television to calculating a math problem, but many others have absolutely no known triggers. Part of what makes epilepsy such a perplexing condition is the way it impacts people with a variety of symptoms and intensities. Even among people with the same seizure syndrome or seizures that affect the same area of the brain, a wide spectrum of seizure frequency and severity exists.

Epilepsy can be a very individualized condition, as two people with the seizure disorder will likely experience it in very different ways. From the convulsions of a tonic-clonic seizure to the stares of an absence seizure, epilepsy can have varied physical impacts on people. The condition takes an emotional toll as well, and people with epilepsy develop their own way of coping with their seizures and the challenges epilepsy brings to their lives.

CHAPTER THREE

Living with Epilepsy

Coming to terms with epilepsy is not a simple matter, but the majority of people with it find some treatment to help them control the seizures. People with epilepsy must deal with a variety of issues associated with the disorder. The seizures are the most obvious physical affliction with which they cope, but in addition are side effects from medication, social acceptance issues, and the limitations that epilepsy places on their lives. There also decisions to be made about treatment if medication does not work. Frustration, resilience, determination, and often patience enter in as they cope with epilepsy's impact on their daily lives.

Mary Woodward: An Unusual Trigger

Her first major seizure was beginning, but Mary Woodward had no idea what was happening. She was studying in the basement of her sorority house, reading a book, when her jaw began to shake so hard that she had to clench her teeth to keep it from moving. Her leg kicked out involuntarily, and her neck began to hurt severely. Still, she did not realize she was about to go into convulsions.

She does not remember falling shaking to the floor or being caught just in time by a friend who kept her from hitting her head. "The last thing I remember is a big, terrible pain in my neck," she says. "Then I blacked out and woke up on the ground with people looking down on me."[24]

The Denver native was a twenty-year-old college student when she had her first major seizure, and the thought that she might have epilepsy had never entered her mind. She is now upfront with her condition, but the diagnosis was initially shocking, scary, and upsetting. When she learned she had epilepsy, her reaction was one of dismay. "At first they thought it was stress, a one-time thing," she says. "Then we went to see a neurologist and she said, 'No, it's not.' They did testing and she said, 'This is genetic, it's in your family.'"[25]

A patient with epilepsy is hooked up to EEG machines so doctors can monitor brain activity and wait for a seizure to occur.

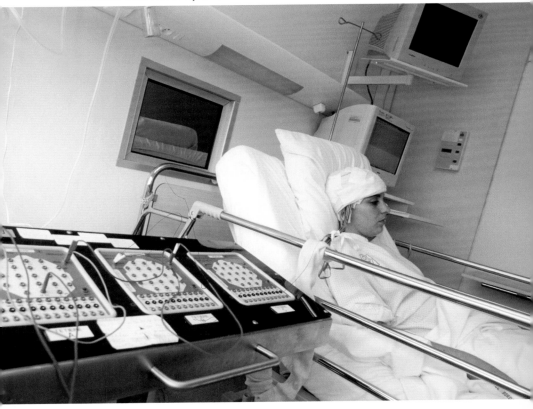

The news was also unsettling to Woodward's family. "My mom and I were crying in the [neurologist's] office," she recalls. "The neurologist asked me if I had hallucinations or out-of-body experiences, and I said, 'I feel like I'm having one now.' It was a surprise, a shock. I couldn't believe it was happening to me. My family was really scared, I think more than anything they couldn't believe it."[26]

Once she became aware of what a seizure was, however, Woodward realized she had been having them several times a week throughout high school without knowing it. "I would stutter, and reading became difficult at some point," she says. "I would get stuck on a word. Sometimes my leg would spasm or my arm would spasm, and I would also have little jaw jerks. It was very strange, but I didn't think too much of it. At the time I just kind of ignored it."[27]

Initially, doctors did not realize that reading triggered her seizures, and Woodward spent five days in the hospital over

Unsuccessful Treatment

Although a number of treatment options exist for people with epilepsy, sometimes a treatment cannot be found. That is the case for Sylvie Lammert, whose father, Warren, and mother, Kathy, and a number of their colleagues began the Epilepsy Therapy Project to find new treatments for epilepsy.

"I have a delightful, loving, spirited, 12-year-old girl who lives with daily waves of seizures and has since she was 1 year old despite having tried literally every relevant available drug, the ketogenic diet and having an implanted medical device," says Warren Lammert, who is the chairman of the Epilepsy Therapy Project and the creator of epilepsy.com. "Despite having the best medical care from a truly committed wonderful doctor, nothing seems to work."

Quoted in National Public Radio, "Living with the Uncertainty of Epilepsy," April 28, 2009. www.npr.org/templates/story/story.php?storyId=103577442.

spring break as doctors tried to find what made them occur. She was hooked up to an EEG machine, and her movements were videotaped as doctors waited for her to have a seizure. She did not have a seizure while she was there, but when Woodward told her doctor that she had been reading before her seizure occurred, the doctor realized that reading was the trigger.

She began taking medication to control her seizures, but the dosage was initially too low. She had another seizure while reading the employee handbook during her first day of work at a mall clothing store. "I was taken out of the mall on a stretcher," she says. "It was humiliating. After that they upped my medicine."[28]

Eventually, the correct dosage of medication was found, and Woodward's seizures became controlled. The twenty-five-year-old works for a New York book publisher and is able to read without incident. Although the medication she takes sometimes makes her sleepy, she is happy to deal with that side effect if it means she will not have seizures. "I hope they find a cure but it's so complicated and underfunded that who knows?" she says. "Maybe not in my lifetime but I love the fact that I know what my trigger is and that I'm able to control it. I consider myself lucky. Everybody has something, this is my something."[29]

B.J. Hamrick: Gaining Social Acceptance

Seizures, migraines, and medication were all part of B.J. Hamrick's life with epilepsy, but they were not the toughest part of dealing with the seizure disorder. What bothered her most was the social awkwardness. "The biggest thing for me was being embarrassed," she says. "I would be staring off into space, and people would be trying to get my attention. The next thing I would be aware of was me coming back and people waving in my face and saying, 'Hello!'"[30]

Hamrick's family began to notice that she would have bouts of inattentiveness when she was ten, but they attributed it to illnesses that followed a rough round of strep throat. For a time, she just could not seem to get completely healthy. "I just couldn't get rid of [the strep throat]," she says. "I kept staying chronically ill after that."[31]

While they were focusing on that aspect of her health, her family did not realize that the North Carolina girl was also showing signs of epilepsy. She would seem to "space out" as her absence seizures went untreated and her family and doctors tried to figure out what was going on. "We thought I actually had a heart problem, because my heart rate would go really high when I was having a seizure," Hamrick says. "Then we went to our family practice doctor and he took one look at one of my episodes and said, 'She's having a seizure.'"[32]

Hamrick was diagnosed with epilepsy at age fourteen and began taking medication to control the seizures. She had to switch to a new medication when she built up resistance to the drug and the seizures returned. "The migraines that went hand in hand with that made it hard to function," she recalls. "It usually happened several times a week, and would be very difficult to get rid of."[33]

Her friends were supportive at first, but as time went on Hamrick's health issues began to impact her social life. Her friends could not seem to understand what was happening to her. "They weren't cruel or mean but they moved on with their lives," she says.

> Here I was struggling to get out of bed in the morning. You're not going to want to hang out with someone who can't even get out of bed. People would assume that if I wasn't feeling well I didn't want to spend time with them. And that wasn't true. I might have some limitations on my energy level, but I still wanted to hang out and do things.[34]

Hamrick's mother began homeschooling the high school student, who did as much as she was able to as she worked around her seizures and migraine episodes. "We did the best we could every day with everything," Hamrick says. Her older brother and sister were supportive of her as she dealt with her health issues. "I know it was hard on them sometimes because I had a lot of extra attention, but they handled it really well," she says. "My sister was really good about standing up for me and explaining things about what was happening to me."[35]

As time went on, she became close to some girls who had come to understand her condition. "I found a core group of friends who didn't mind my limitations and wanted to hang out with me for my personality," she says. "Most were people I had grown up with and they had watched my journey."[36]

Hamrick finished high school, although it took her a little longer than others because of her health issues. She enrolled in college, found a job as a receptionist, and was pleasantly surprised when she noticed that the migraine and seizure episodes were lessening. Eventually, the seizures stopped completely. She had outgrown her epilepsy.

"I was twenty-one when I had my last recognizable seizure. I only get a migraine maybe once or twice a year," says Hamrick, now twenty-five. "The neurologist declared me seizure-free at twenty-two. For a while you're kind of like looking over your shoulder and you think they're going to come back. Then after a while you start to really believe it."[37]

It was difficult to have epilepsy, she acknowledges, and she encourages those with the condition not to lose hope that things will improve. "My biggest thing would be not to give up," says Hamrick, who graduated from college with a degree in journalism and is a freelance writer. "When you're in the middle of it, it feels like it's not going to end and your whole life has come to a stop. My advice would be to just hang in there."[38]

Alex Cooper: Living with Limitations

Alex Cooper does not remember his first seizure, but he does remember being surprised when he woke up in an ambulance. "They said, 'You just had a seizure,'" the fourteen-year-old from Maryland says. "I was shocked. I didn't know what a seizure was."[39]

He was only nine when he had his first seizure, but Alex soon became more familiar with seizures than he wanted to be. By fourteen, he has had too many to count. "When I have a seizure, I kind of wake up making a gagging noise, or just a weird noise coming out of my mouth," he says. "After that my body starts to shake. I have no control of my body and I can't feel anything. If I try to say anything, it slurs my words. That's the most annoying part of the seizure because I can't call for help."[40]

Alex's first seizure came during an overnight Boy Scout camping trip, when he had trouble sleeping because of cold weather. Later, an overnight EEG test at the hospital that looked at his brain waves found his seizures came when he was overtired. He also learned that he has a genetic condition that makes him susceptible to getting the seizures.

A patient with epilepsy is monitored overnight in an effort to make an epilepsy diagnosis.

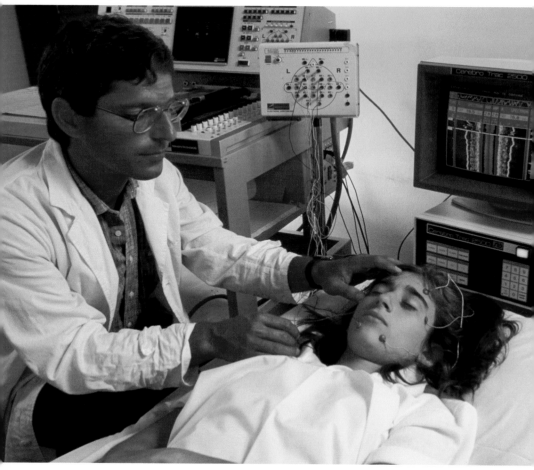

Staying on a routine sleep schedule is an important part of managing his seizures, and that was no problem when he was first diagnosed. When Alex learned that his seizures were triggered by being tired, he did not want to take any chances at not getting enough sleep. "I wanted to go to bed every night at like eight or seven," he says. "I didn't want to have another seizure."[41]

Because his seizures happen when he is sleeping, Alex takes medication only in the early evening. The medication gradually wears off during the day, and he is not supposed to nap. He learned the danger of doing so one day when he lay down on the couch with a migraine headache. He fell asleep and went into a seizure. "All of [a] sudden I heard my mom screaming in the phone," he says. "I was having a seizure and I turned blue."[42]

That seizure lasted for several minutes and was his most severe one. His seizures are usually brief, but they do not seem quick to him. "When I have a seizure, I'll have one that's maybe three seconds or ten seconds, but to me it feels like an hour," Alex says. "Afterwards I'm fully awake but I can't really control my speaking, and my left arm goes totally numb."[43]

Medication makes his seizures less severe, but getting the right dosage can be a challenge. Growth spurts make it difficult to keep the dosage accurate. "Every time I gain a lot of weight and get taller, the medicine won't work for me,"[44] he explains.

Having seizures was scary initially, but the teen now finds his epilepsy to be more frustrating than frightening. He has had to miss an overnight class camping trip and decline to go on vacations with a friend because he fears others will not know what to do if he has a seizure away from home. He also has had to turn down an invitation to participate in a student ambassador program to Australia and a school trip to France because the travel would interrupt his sleep schedule and could bring on a seizure.

The good news for Alex is that he has a type of epilepsy called benign rolandic epilepsy, which a person typically outgrows. His seizures have been becoming less frequent, and he remains optimistic by focusing on the future. "I just think of the day I get the news that I'm seizure-free," he says. "There are so many fun things I've wanted to do. One of my friends says during our senior year we'll go backpacking through Europe, so I hope I don't have seizures by then. I really want to go more places."[45]

Heather Good: Ready to Try a New Treatment

Heather Good, a nineteen-year-old from Florida, has spent much of her life searching for a way to make her seizures go away. She has tried to control them with medication and surgery, and although she has experienced some periods of relief, the seizures always return. The college student looks forward to being a nurse one day, but she is still searching for the treatment that will finally rid her of seizures forever.

Good was only two years old when her mother noticed that her body would get stiff just as she was falling asleep. She was hospitalized as doctors looked for a cause; while there, she suffered a seizure. Doctors diagnosed her with epilepsy. "I don't know how often I had them, but they always happened when I was going to sleep," Good says. "During the day I never have them . . . I've been on medication since I was two," she adds. "A lot of the medications haven't fully worked; they're not fully controlling my seizures."[46]

Good's seizures occur while she is sleeping. Her body tenses and sometimes shakes for about a minute. Heather stays sleeping during her seizure, but in the morning she is tired and groggy.

Because medication was not taking her seizures away, Good and her family began to look at other treatment options. When Good was thirteen they decided to try surgery that would remove the part of Heather's brain that was causing the seizures. Before she had that surgery, however, doctors first needed to pinpoint the part of her brain causing her seizures. Good had an internal EEG, which involved a surgery to have electrodes placed on the surface of her brain. The electrodes would detect her brain waves and show where the seizure activity was occurring. Once they knew which area of her brain was having

A Rock Star with Epilepsy

In April 2009 the rock star Prince admitted publicly for the first time that he had had epilepsy as a child. "I used to have seizures when I was young. My mother and father didn't know what to do or how to handle it, but they did the best they could with what little they had," he said in an interview on the *Tavis Smiley* show on PBS.

Prince said that because of his epilepsy, he had to deal with getting teased in school. The fact that he had epilepsy also influenced his musical career and performing style. "Early in my career I tried to compensate for that by being as flashy as I could and as noisy as I could," he said.

Quoted in *Tavis Smiley*, "Prince," April 27, 2009. www.pbs.org/kcet/tavissmiley/archive/200904/20090427_prince.html.

Rock musician Prince revealed in 2009 that he suffered from epilepsy as a child.

the seizures, doctors then did more tests to see if that area controlled any vital functions. "[During the tests] they give you a book to read, turn off something in your brain, and all of [a] sudden I couldn't read any more," Good says. "Or I was talking and I couldn't talk anymore."[47]

The tests showed that she had some speech and motor skills in the area where her seizures began. Surgeons could not remove the entire area, but they could safely take out some of it. The prospect of having brain surgery and a portion of her brain removed did not make Good nervous. Rather, she was excited about the possibility of having something take away her seizures. And for a time, the surgery did. "I noticed a difference for about six months after that," Good says. "Since then I haven't noticed as much of a difference."[48]

Twice a day, Good takes three medications for her seizures. Rather than becoming less frequent, though, they have been occurring more and more often. The nineteen-year-old often has seizures just as she is falling asleep or waking up. Good sometimes worries that her seizures will never go away or that she will have one in a public place, but she is determined not to let them define her. "I can't let my life be totally consumed by seizures and my epilepsy and how to stop it," she says. "Sometimes I tell people that epilepsy is not me, it's only one part of me. I can't let it rule my life."[49]

A surgeon removes brain tissue from a young girl's brain to alleviate her seizure symptoms.

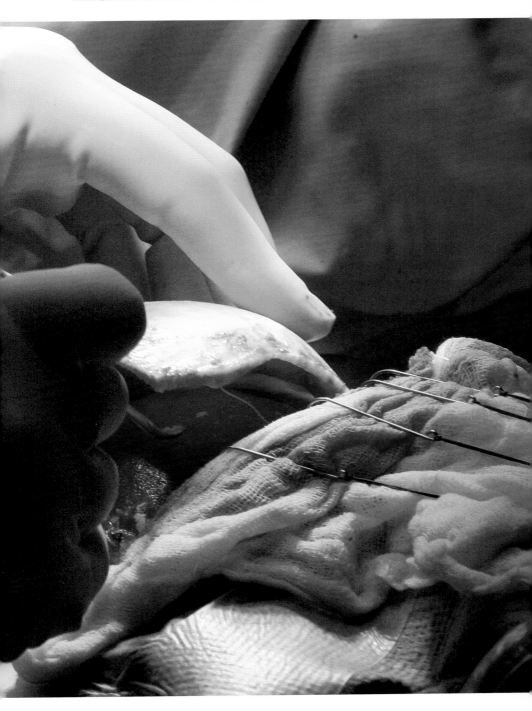

Good has found it easier to cope with her epilepsy as she has gotten older. A teen group, sponsored by the Epilepsy Foundation, helped her to realize that she was not the only person whose life was impacted by seizures:

> For a long time before I joined the teen group I was ashamed of it. I was afraid of what people would think. I didn't tell people about it unless they were really close friends. But when I joined the teen group I realized that there is so much stigma surrounding epilepsy because people never talk about it, and I'm hurting the cause when I don't talk about it.[50]

Although she is no longer ashamed to have epilepsy, Good still finds aspects of her condition frustrating. She began attending college and plans to go into pediatric nursing, but she wishes she did not have to watch her sleep schedule quite as closely as she does. "It's kind of frustrating in that way because I have to stop and take care of myself," she says. "It's especially hard in college, when you want to stay up and get work done."[51]

Good continues to look for something that will completely control her seizures. She is trying the Atkins diet, which she hopes will work on the same principles as the high-fat, low-carb ketogenic diet that has worked in children with epilepsy. She is also considering being part of a medical trial for a device implanted in the brain that detects seizures before they begin and uses a shock to stop them. She believes it is important for people with epilepsy to continue searching for answers. "If you sit around and pout about it, it's not going to do anything, that's my outlook," she says. "If you try to find answers and try new clinical trials and meet people with epilepsy and network, it's going to be way better for you than if you just sit around. Some people just settle, and in my mind that's not OK."[52]

Noel Johnson: Getting Her Life Back

At age twenty-three, Noel Johnson is an upbeat newlywed with a degree in marketing, a diploma in nursing, and an optimistic view of the future. As a teen, however, her energy level was drained by seizures and the medication that she took to control them. "I would take my medicine at 9:00 A.M. or noon, and if I was not on the couch within thirty minutes, I was so dizzy I couldn't walk," she says. "I was homeschooled, so that was a blessing, but it was still really hard."[53]

The seizures that dramatically impacted Johnson's life began early in her teen years, and at first she thought she was going crazy. One minute she would be fine, the next she could not figure out where she was. At first, her family blamed these feelings on the flu or another illness. When she was fifteen, however, the episodes became much worse. "I was just bombarded," she says. "One minute I knew where I was, and the next minute I had to reassure myself that I was Noel . . . and that I was in my living room and my mom was sitting next to me and this is the house I had always lived in."[54]

Johnson's seizures were worse when she was tired, but they could happen any time. She would have no warning that they were about to begin. After visiting the doctor, Johnson and her family learned that her disoriented feeling was a form of epilepsy and that her seizures were beginning deep in the brain. Medication controlled the seizures for a while, but the side effects had a major impact on Johnson's energy level. "By my senior year I was like a zombie,"[55] she says.

Johnson's seizures and her reaction to the medication had a significant impact on the way she was able to live her life, as it severely limited her energy level and what she was able to do. "My friends never said anything or criticized me, but it was one of those things that was just hard," she recalls. "I just physically couldn't do it. I was tired, and I just wasn't there. The medicine controls the seizures, but then you have the drowsiness and the dizziness coupled with the seizures. That made it hard to live a normal life."[56]

Johnson reached the maximum dosage for two medications, but at age seventeen her seizures were still coming. She would experience as many as fifteen to thirty seizures a day and was becoming depressed about her situation. Her seizures were not going away, and her reaction to the medication was severe.

Surgery to remove the part of her brain causing the seizures was not an option. "My seizures are so deep in the brain that even if I wanted to do brain surgery it would do more damage than good,"[57] Johnson says. There was another alternative, however. Johnson and her family decided to try an option called vagus nerve stimulation.

Vagus nerve stimulation (VNS) uses small doses of electrical energy to try to rid a person of seizures. To get this electrical energy to the brain, a small device is inserted under the skin of a patient's chest. A wire leads from the device to the vagus nerve in the neck. The nerve takes the electrical energy produced by the battery-operated device to the brain. "They don't go into the brain, that's the amazing part," Johnson says. "The surgery wasn't bad at all. It was outpatient surgery, and I was able to go home that day. Because everything is under the skin, I don't have to worry about infection or not being able to swim."[58]

The device changed her life dramatically. Her seizures dropped to one or two a week, she was able to cut down on her medication, and she no longer got sleepy during the day. Her entire outlook changed. "I was able to laugh again and enjoy life,"[59] the Florida woman says.

The treatment also broadened her career options and allowed her to enjoy new experiences. "There are so many things I wouldn't be able to do if I had not had VNS therapy," says Johnson, who works as a nanny and hopes to one day work with children with epilepsy. "It's a huge blessing from the Lord. It's like my medical miracle. My quality of life is completely different. I have confidence now. I'm able to stay awake and enjoy life."[60]

Johnson knows firsthand how difficult and disheartening it can be to struggle with epilepsy, and she has seen discouragement among others with epilepsy who are trying to cope with seizures and the side effects of medication. She urges others with epilepsy to persevere, noting that she was able to make it through school despite the fact that she had problems with her memory. "I was determined," she says.

You might not make an A, but you're going to make a B. Keep going forward. If you have to take a class two times, you're going to pass it the second time. A lot of times you

A Vagus Nerve Stimulator, or VNS, is inserted under the chest skin and is then attached to the vagus nerve in the neck.

don't understand why you have epilepsy, but God has a plan for you. Just keep going. Try new treatments. If you think diet might help, try diet; if you think VNS might work for you, try that. It is hard, but there is hope out there, there are answers and there are more options.[61]

CHAPTER FOUR

Tests and Treatments for Epilepsy

The goal of epilepsy treatment is to get a person to stop having seizures. Many different treatments are needed because of the myriad causes of epilepsy and the individual needs of each patient. Treatment strategies include medication, surgery, implanted devices, and other methods, which all have the same goal of getting seizures under control.

An EEG

When deciding how to treat a person with epilepsy, doctors attempt to find what causes the seizures to occur. Information about the way the seizure impacts a person's body and which parts of the brain are involved in the seizure all help a doctor find the appropriate treatment.

The first test a person typically undergoes when epilepsy is suspected is an electroencephalograph (EEG). The electroencephalograph is a machine that has been around since the 1920s and is used to monitor a person's brain waves. The brain waves can offer important information and clues about a person's seizures. Although the brain's electrical activity is not visible, an EEG machine uses sensors to detect the brain's electrical impulses and translates this electrical activity into a set of squiggly lines. These lines are displayed on a computer monitor or are printed on a strip of paper. The EEG readout allows a doctor to take a look at the electrical activity going on in a person's brain.

Having an EEG test is a safe and painless procedure. To gather information about the electrical activity inside a person's brain, the EEG device uses electrodes placed on a person's scalp. A number of electrodes, which are small metal disks, are attached to the scalp and have wires that are connected to an electrical box that records the brain's electrical activity. The wires do not bring an electrical current to the scalp; instead, they simply record the electrical activity going on in the brain. The electrical box is connected to an EEG ma-

A person undergoes an electroencephalograph (EEG), which monitors brain waves and electrical activity in the brain.

chine, which translates the electrical activity in the brain into a set of visible lines, called traces.

The lines on the EEG readout provide information about different areas of the brain. A doctor can interpret the lines to determine if these areas are producing a normal EEG readout or if there are abnormalities that may be caused by seizures. "If it is abnormal, you can tell what kind of epilepsy someone might be having," says Sanjay Singh, director of the Nebraska Epilepsy Center. "It can also tell you where in the brain the seizure might be."[62]

A Normal EEG

Although certain brain wave patterns indicate that a person is likely to have epilepsy, about half of the time the EEG indicates a normal brain wave pattern. This does not mean that the person does not have epilepsy, however. Abnormal brain waves may only occur during a seizure, and if a person is tested when a seizure is not occurring, the brain waves may look normal.

If the EEG looks normal, the doctor will use other information to make a diagnosis of epilepsy. A description of the seizure, provided by the person being tested or a friend or relative who saw the seizure, is important. A person's medical history, which would include information about head injuries or illnesses that may have caused an infection in the brain, is another tool used by doctors when diagnosing epilepsy.

The MEG

A newer technique, the magnetoencephalograph (MEG), is also used to look at brain activity and help pinpoint the location of a seizure. The electrical currents in the brain produce tiny magnetic fields, and the MEG provides a picture of what these magnetic fields look like. "We've been recording electrical activity of the brain for eighty or ninety years now, and we should have figured out there is also magnetic activity generated by these brain cells," Singh says. "This is one of the best epilepsy evaluation advances in the last decade or so."[63]

The MEG is more accurate than the EEG, as it produces a better picture of brain activity. The skull and brain tissue do not impact the MEG as much as they do the EEG, and the MEG offers more detail. "Instead of the 20-channel EEG, this is 306 channels," Singh says. "It is so accurate that if you move your index finger, it will tell you exactly from where in the brain the movement came from."[64]

The information gathered from the MEG is combined with information about the brain's structure, which is provided by magnetic resonance imaging (MRI). The MRI uses a powerful magnet to produce an image. A person may also have a computed tomography (CT) scan. The scan uses a low amount of radiation to get a picture of the brain, although the picture quality is not as high as the image produced by an MRI. Together, these tools help identify the areas of the brain that may be the source of the seizures.

Other Monitoring Tests

If an EEG and other tests do not provide sufficient information to make the diagnosis, a doctor will sometimes employ video EEG monitoring. During this monitoring, a person comes into the epilepsy unit in the hospital and stays in a room equipped with a video camera. For several days the patient has EEG sensors stuck to his or her scalp, which record brain wave activity. Because the sensors and video are always on, any seizures that occur during the hospitalization will be captured by the machines, helping the doctor to make a diagnosis.

Another technique for studying brain waves and pinpointing the source of a seizure is the use of intracranial electrodes. These electrodes are placed inside the brain during a six- or seven-hour operation. After they are in place, they measure a patient's brain activity at hundreds of points.

Treatment

Although these tests do not always show the cause of a person's epilepsy, they do provide information that a doctor uses to help the patient decide on the best course of treatment. Treatment for epilepsy aims to rid a person of seizures or cut down on the number of seizures a person has. When people are treated for epilepsy, about 80 percent do not have seizures for at least two

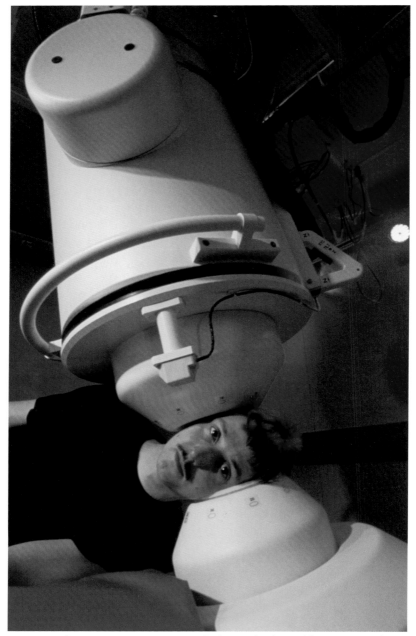

A man undergoes a magnetoencephalography (MEG) brain scan. The MEG is more accurate than the EEG and gives a clearer image of brain activity.

years or often longer, and about half are seizure free after taking their first antiseizure medication. "The chances of becoming completely seizure-free are best if there is no known brain injury or abnormality, and if the person has a normal neurological examination and EEG,"[65] notes Steven Schachter, a professor of neurology at Harvard Medical School.

Because epilepsy is caused by so many different things, many medications and other methods are used to treat it. Epilepsy is a very individualized disorder, and no single treatment works in every person who has epilepsy. "Partly because there are so many different causes, we will never have one treatment or one cure that will help everybody with epilepsy," says Roy Sucholeiki of Central DuPage Hospital in Chicago. "For the vast majority of people there is no cure, rather there is treatment. Cures are for a tumor that can be removed, or in a small percentage of people with epilepsy, it can be localized to some part of the brain that can be targeted for brain surgery."[66]

Medication

Surgery is typically not the initial course of treatment that is tried in a patient with epilepsy, however. The first line of treatment for epilepsy typically is medication, to which 60 to 70 percent of patients respond. "Medicines have come out in the last couple of years that are so well tolerated and safe that it's the first line of treatment,"[67] Sucholeiki says.

Since the 1980s, the medication options for people with epilepsy have dramatically improved, Sucholeiki adds. There are more than twenty drug treatments for epilepsy, including Keppra, Zarontin, and Lamictal. As Sanjay Singh notes, "Fifteen or twenty years ago we only had four or five drugs to treat patients. The last ten or fifteen years we've had another ten to twelve medications."[68]

Doctors can use a single medication to treat a patient or can combine drugs to give the patient the best chance of being seizure free. It is not always clear which combination is best until the patient tries it, however. "I can look at a person, do all the testing, even see their seizure, and I can't tell which drug they'll respond to," says Carl Bazil, the leader of the Columbia

Comprehensive Epilepsy Center, which is part of the Columbia University Medical Center. "There must be something about their action in the brain, but we don't know what that is."[69]

Drug Treatment Side Effects

Epilepsy drugs may carry serious side effects that vary from person to person and medication to medication. One patient may become lethargic and be extremely tired after taking epilepsy medication. Another medication may cause a person to become hyperactive and unable to settle down. Other side effects can include gaining or losing weight as well as becoming dizzy or anemic. Osteoporosis or mental disturbances are other potential side effects. When prescribing epilepsy medication, doctors must balance the benefits of the drug treatment with the problems it may cause. Epilepsy expert Orrin Devinsky of New York University explains:

> You might have two staring spells a month lasting a couple of minutes, and you're on a high dose of medication. Now, I can put you on a second medication and get you down to one a month. So now you've got two extra minutes a month but in exchange it's affecting your quality of life for the 15 hours a day you're awake: it may make you tired or dizzy, or cause mood changes or memory problems. So do you want to make that trade-off?[70]

Surgery

Despite its side effects, medication is often an effective treatment for more than half of people with epilepsy. However, about 30 to 40 percent of people with epilepsy continue to have seizures even though they are taking medication. A person who does not respond to medication must consider other ways to stop the seizures; typically, the next treatment option is surgery. During surgery, the part of the brain causing the seizures is removed, leaving the healthy tissue.

Much work is done before surgery to make sure that the portion being removed does not control vital functions. Before surgery, a person goes through an extensive evaluation as the

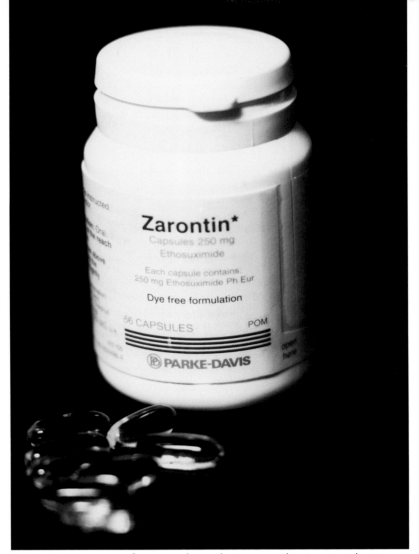

Zarontin is just one of twenty drugs that are used to treat epileptic symptoms.

surgeon tries to pinpoint the exact part of the brain that is causing the seizure. Testing is necessary because the precise location is not always apparent by sight or touch during surgery. "If there is a brain tumor or a major developmental malformation you can see or feel there's something wrong, but in the majority of the cases there's nothing really to be seen,"[71] Singh says.

In addition to EEG monitoring and an MRI scan, a person also undergoes neuropsychological testing before surgery to

Interpreting an EEG

In addition to seizures, abnormal EEG readouts can be caused by conditions related to head trauma, strokes, or brain tumors. Some brain wave patterns are typical of epilepsy, however. If a doctor sees spikes and sharp waves on an EEG readout, they may indicate that the part of the brain producing this activity is the source of a person's seizures.

Figuring out exactly what the bumpy lines on an EEG readout mean is a skill acquired by trained neurologists, who know which types of lines signal abnormalities and which changes in the readout are caused by things such as patients opening their eyes or closing their mouths. A doctor also takes other information about a patient into account when looking at the EEG. "Interpreting EEGs also involves some subjectivity and judgment," notes Steven Schachter, a professor of neurology at Harvard Medical School. "What one interpreter reads as sharp waves may be read as spikes by another. Both may be considered correct, depending on the criteria they apply. Experienced neurologists also learn to interpret the EEG in light of the patient's medical history, physical examination, and other laboratory studies."

Steven Schachter, "Where It's Performed," *Epilepsy.com*. www.epilepsy.com/epilepsy/eeg_where.

measure memory, language, and other skills. These tests can help doctors determine which part of the brain is not functioning properly. The surgeon can also use a positron emission tomography scan to see how well the brain uses glucose, as an area that is not using glucose well could be the site of a person's seizures. A magnetoencephalograph scan can also be used to measure brain activity and provide doctors with a three-dimensional map of the brain. A SPECT (single photon emission computerized tomography) scan, which looks at blood flow in the brain, is another evaluation tool doctors may use. "The blood is sent to the most active regions of the brain,"

Singh explains. "The most blood will be going toward that region with a seizure."[72]

If these tests show that a patient is likely to be helped by surgery, more information is gathered. The Wada test may be used to see whether memory is impaired on one side of the brain. The test involves having a catheter inserted into an artery in the groin, which carries a drug to the brain that puts that half of the brain to sleep so the other side of the brain can be tested for memory and language. The test is then repeated for the other side of the brain. The test will show if memory on one side of the brain has been affected, and it also shows whether the brain can be operated on without harming memory.

A technique called brain mapping can also be used to determine if the area targeted for surgery controls vital functions such as speech, sight, or movement. While much general information is known about where these functions are located in the brain,

Doctors prepare a patient for brain surgery to implant electrodes under the skull. These electrodes will stimulate certain parts of the brain.

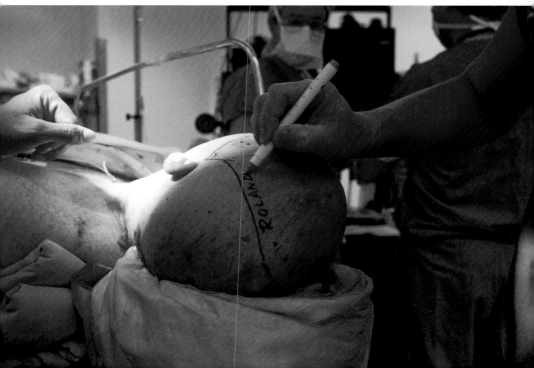

many variations occur, so it is important to determine where these functions lie in a person's brain before surgery is done. "The exact location of various functions differs quite a bit from person to person," notes Dr. Howard L. Weiner, a professor at New York University Langone Medical Center. "The presence of tumors, seizures, or other brain abnormalities may distort these maps so that general rules do not apply."[73]

Electrical stimulation of various parts of the brain can be used to see where the vital functions are located. If the area where the seizures are starting is difficult to detect with a test using electrodes on the outside of the skull, or if the area is close to a critical functioning area, a doctor can also perform surgery to place a grid of electrodes under the skull, directly onto the surface of the brain, to gather information. Depth electrodes that go more deeply into the brain can also be used to help map functions. A small amount of electrical current is sent to the electrodes to determine which functions are controlled by these areas. If a person has trouble speaking, for example, when the current is sent to a specific area, then it indicates that the area likely controls speech.

Tests Are Not Always Needed

Although brain-imaging tests such as magnetic resonance imaging (MRI) or computed tomography (CT) scans can be helpful to doctors in diagnosing epilepsy, there are times when they are not used. When it is clear that a person has a certain type of epilepsy, the scans are not ordered because their results are almost always normal. "Many doctors will not order a CT or MRI scan for patients with certain well-defined epilepsy syndromes that are often genetic," notes Ruben Kuzniecky, a professor at New York University School of Medicine.

Ruben Kuzniecky, "Looking at the Brain," *Epilepsy.com.* www.epilepsy.com/EPILEPSY/looking_brain.

During surgery, a doctor removes the part of the brain that is causing the seizures or removes the areas of the brain containing nerve pathways that seizures follow as they spread. Surgery is not a guarantee that a person's seizures will stop, although some patients are free of seizures after surgery. Improvement is typically seen, however. "Many people fall between these extremes, having fewer seizures or seizures that are less intense, or they require less medication," Weiner says. "Most people who do become seizure-free after surgery must continue to take seizure medicines (though often at lower dosages) to prevent breakthrough seizures."[74]

Vagus Nerve Stimulation

A patient who does not respond to medication and is not a good candidate for surgery has other options for seizure control. One of these is vagus nerve stimulation (VNS). The VNS device has been called a pacemaker for the brain, and it sends a mild, brief electrical pulse to the vagus nerve in the neck every few seconds or minutes. The nerve carries the electrical pulse to the brain. It turns off and on automatically; the person using it usually does not even realize that it is there.

The brain is impacted by the VNS's electrical pulse, but implanting the VNS device does not require brain surgery because the device is implanted in the chest and is connected to a nerve in the neck. Exactly how the VNS reduces seizures is a mystery. Although it is not considered a cure, the device provides relief for some patients. "About 50 percent of people with VNS find that their seizure problem is improved 50 percent," Sucholeiki says. "It's not the be all and end all, but it can be tried when drugs haven't worked. It's a very safe procedure."[75]

For James Sandstedt of Texas, the VNS has been a life-changing device. Before the seventeen-year-old had the device implanted, he was averaging more than one hundred seizures a night and was extremely lethargic. The high school junior has been able to reduce the amount of medication he takes and is now able to enjoy activities he never had the energy for when he was heavily medicated and suffering from numerous seizures. "Before I wasn't really alive, I was just existing," he says. "Now I actually have a life."[76] His mother cannot believe the difference she has seen in her son:

> When he had the VNS surgery it was like night and day. He's having the life he never had before. There was a time I didn't think he would make it, he was having so many seizures in one day. He would not walk half a block, and was so exhausted when he would come home from school all he did was sleep. Then he had the VNS. Now he has energy, which he never had before.[77]

Diet Treatment

Another method used to control epilepsy is diet. Some children are able to control their seizures with the ketogenic diet, which is high in fat but extremely low in carbohydrates. It is not known exactly how this works, but it has been effective in some cases.

With this diet, a person eats four times as much fat as carbohydrates and protein. It has a low sugar content, which may prevent seizures from forming in the brain. This diet can be complicated, however, and difficult to follow. "You're pretty much eating protein and fat," Singh says. "It is useful, but it can have other consequences, so this is the final option. It's a very cumbersome thing to do, and certainly requires a lot of dedication and discipline."[78]

Another diet that has shown some promise is a modified Atkins diet. This diet includes many high-fat foods, such as bacon, cheese, and whipping cream. The amount of carbohydrates, such as bread and cake, is limited. Studies have shown that two-thirds of patients on the diet were able to reduce the number of seizures they had.

Becoming Seizure Free

Diet, medication, surgery, or an implanted device may help a person become free of seizures, or reduce their number of seizures. A person who has seizures as a child may outgrow them; about half of children who have epilepsy are taken off medication after several years. "It's likely that one way people

A ketogenic diet is a carefully proportioned diet high in fat and low in carbohydrates and is credited with reducing epileptic seizures in children.

outgrow it is that the childhood brain is prone to excess electrical activity," Sucholeiki says. "As the brain matures, it has its own mechanisms to dampen the excessive activity."[79]

For those whose epilepsy cannot be cured, seizure control is the goal. "Most people with epilepsy will live normal lives once their seizures are controlled,"[80] Sanjay Singh notes. However, this control is elusive for some people with epilepsy. These patients are still waiting for a treatment that will cure or curb their seizures and allow them to live a life without worrying about the next storm in their brain.

CHAPTER FIVE

The Future of Epilepsy

Although progress has been made in how epilepsy is treated, work still needs to be done. The majority of people with epilepsy have their seizures under control, but the Epilepsy Foundation estimates that 10 percent of new patients fail to get control of their seizures, even with medical intervention. Seventy percent of people with epilepsy enter remission and are seizure free for five years are more, but that leaves 30 percent who are still searching for a solution. For thousands of people, epilepsy remains a frustrating barrier to a normal life.

Many questions about seizures remain unanswered. It is known that epilepsy is caused by uncontrolled electrical activity in the brain, but what causes this activity and the workings of the brain continue to remain mysteries. Treatments have been able to stop some seizures, but there is much more to be learned about epilepsy itself. "Treatments are band aids designed to treat the expression of the disorder," notes William Davis Gaillard, the division chief of epilepsy and neurophysiology at Children's National Medical Center in Washington, D.C., "but they do not treat the underlying disorder."[81]

Currently no sure cure exists for epilepsy, although some people have their seizures stop or decrease as time goes on. For those who have their seizures controlled by medication, the side effects of fatigue or dizziness can be frustrating. Researchers are looking at new ways to treat epilepsy and determine its causes as they search for answers and a cure that has so far been elusive.

Genetic Research

One way researchers hope to learn more about epilepsy is by studying the genetic makeup of people with epilepsy. Genes carry instructions for determining how our bodies are built, and some genes are associated with disorders. The Epilepsy Phenome/Genome Project, sponsored by the National Institutes of Health and the National Institute of Neurological Disorders and Stroke, is working to identify genes that contribute to a person developing epilepsy. It is also looking at how certain genes respond to seizure medications.

To gather the genetic information, researchers collect blood samples from people who have certain types of epilepsy as well as brothers and sisters who both have epilepsy. They also gather information about people's seizure histories. Researchers hope the information provided through this study will lead to an understanding of the chemical processes in the body that lead to epilepsy as well as improvements in diagnosis and treatment. The information the study provides will help doctors decide which drugs will be most effective and have the fewest side effects for a patient. "It could allow us to match safety and effectiveness of a drug to a specific person, focus research on new therapeutic targets, and crack the code on the causes of common forms of epilepsy,"[82] says Orrin Devinsky, a professor of neurology at the New York University School of Medicine.

Genetic technology has the potential to unlock the cause for epilepsy in a number of cases. Although knowing the genetic makeup of epilepsy will make treatments more effective, Gaillard estimates it could take decades before that happens. One day, however, it may be possible to treat the gene that causes problems in a significant number of people with epilepsy rather than use medication to treat the seizure. "The genetics revolution is going to change how we view epilepsy," he says.

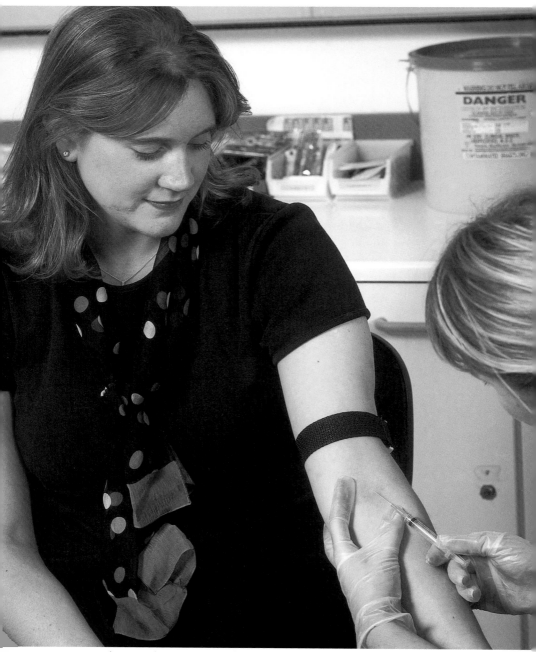

Researchers gather genetic information on epilepsy patients and their relatives in order to better understand the genetics behind epilepsy.

"Eventually we will be able to identify patients at risk for side effects from certain medications and it will also allow us to be more precise in knowing which medications will work for a certain child rather than the random way we treat children now."[83]

Medication Advances

While research is being done to help doctors match an epilepsy patient with the right medication, research is also being done to improve the medications available. Epilepsy medications often come with unwanted side effects, and researchers are looking into new drug treatments that reduce seizures without producing significant side effects.

At the University of Wisconsin—Madison, researchers are trying to create a drug that will mimic the low-sugar diet that some people have found to be effective in reducing seizures. They are using a compound with a chemical structure similar to sugar that blocks sugar metabolism in the brain and prevents the body from using glucose. The cells think they are taking in glucose, but the compound stops them from actually doing so. Tom Sutala, one of the researchers, calls the drug "remarkably safe." He says, "It's about as close to a natural product as you can get without being a natural product."[84]

Changes in the way a drug is delivered may also change in the future. Epilepsy medications are typically in pill form, which causes the medication to travel through the organs and the rest of the body to get to the brain. A new method of delivering medication would deliver the medicine directly to the brain. To get the medication there, a treatment pump or another device would send the drug or an electrical signal to the area in the brain where a person's seizures develop.

Tests are being done with the responsive neurostimulator system, which is a battery-controlled device programmed to detect a seizure before it begins. The brain changes in subtle ways prior to a seizure. It is hoped that the device will sense these changes so that medication or an electrical signal can be sent before the seizure begins and stop it before it starts.

Deep Brain Stimulation

Another treatment being studied is deep brain stimulation, which has been used to treat illnesses such as Parkinson's disease. The treatment uses an electrode implanted in the brain to deliver a pulse to the brain. There are some questions about which areas to stimulate, however, and the treatment has varied results in people with epilepsy.

The treatment involves risks, including a chance of brain bleeding, but it has an advantage over surgery because it does not destroy brain tissue. "The stimulator can be adjusted to achieve the best outcome," notes Howard L. Weiner. "It can also be turned off or removed if adverse side effects occur."[85]

Surgical Advances

Advancements are also being made in surgical instruments used in brain surgery. One advancement for epilepsy patients undergoing surgery is the gamma knife. The instrument can be used to treat seizures that are focused in certain areas of the brain. "Instead of cutting pieces of the brain out, you can burn them through radiation,"[86] Sanjay Singh explains.

Although it is called a knife, the instrument actually uses targeted beams of radiation to remove a tumor or area of the brain. No incision is made; rather, doctors focus beams of radiation on the area of the brain that needs to be removed, thus protecting the surrounding tissue from harm. The procedure allows a patient to avoid having part of the skull removed to allow a surgeon to reach the brain, but it can include side effects, including headaches and depression.

Brain-Imaging Advances

Surgeons are aided by machines that allow them to look inside the brain, and advancements are also being made in the tools that give doctors a more detailed picture of the structure of a person's brain. Improvements in magnetic resonance imaging (MRI) machines are giving doctors a clearer image of what things look like beneath the skull. As the MRI machines become more powerful, they produce images that can show more

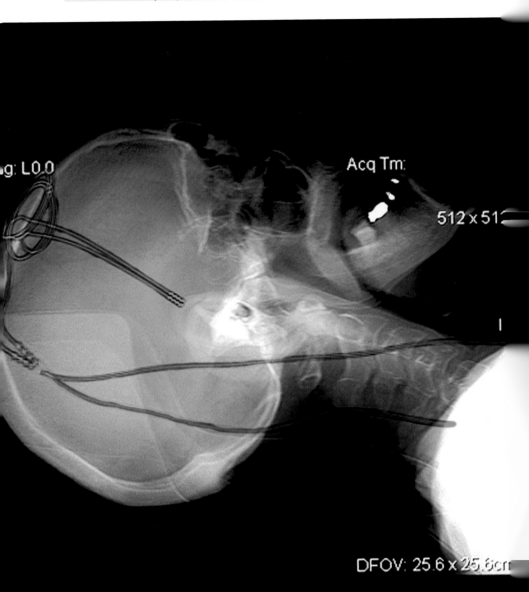

This X-ray shows the placement of two electrodes (green) that extend deep into the brain. This technique, called deep brain stimulation, is used as a treatment for epilepsy and Parkinson's disease.

subtle abnormalities in a person's brain. Using an increased number of different MRI sequences provides doctors such as William Davis Gaillard with more data to use. "More information can be gleaned from those kinds of technologies, and that is only going to increase over the next few years,"[87] he says.

The strength of the magnet in the imaging device is measured in teslas, with many community hospitals having an MRI of 1.5 tesla. An epilepsy center generally has a stronger imaging device of 3 tesla or even 6 tesla. "The stronger the magnet, the better the pictures,"[88] says Singh, who is hopeful that the future brings magnets of 9 tesla. The clearer picture of a person's brain will give doctors more information about where seizures originate and help identify areas to avoid during an operation.

Experiments with Magnetic Activity

The transcranial magnetic stimulator is a nonsurgical treatment currently under study. This very experimental treatment uses a strong magnet to impact a patient's seizures. "By magnetic activity you can stimulate or inhibit areas of the brain,"[89] Singh says.

This procedure involves an electromagnetic coil placed on an area of the head. The coil is switched on and off to produce pulses. Several treatments are usually done. Transcranial magnetic stimulation is also being used as an experimental treatment for depression, and some side effects noted in that treatment include headaches and lightheadedness.

Challenges

Although many exciting advancements are being made in the tools used to diagnose epilepsy and the medications used to treat it, one of the challenges to finding a cure for epilepsy is money. There is an estimated thirty-five dollars in public and private funding for research for each patient, an amount that significantly lags behind funding for other neurological disorders. There are 3 million people living with epilepsy, and some question the level of funding for epilepsy research. "The investment in research by the federal government and the investment of private dollars in epilepsy research have simply not

A new nonsurgical treatment for epilepsy involves the use of magnets. Called the transcranial magnetic stimulator (TMS), the treatment inhibits or stimulates areas of the brain.

been proportional to the burden of the disease,"[90] says Susan Axelrod, whose daughter, Lauren, began suffering epileptic seizures at seven months old.

Eager to see advancements made in epilepsy treatment, Axelrod and others whose lives have been impacted by the disease founded Citizens United for Research in Epilepsy (CURE). The organization raises money and supports researchers looking for a cure for epilepsy. "We want complete freedom from seizures," Axelrod says. "We want future families to be spared what so many other families, for so many years, have endured. Lives should not be defined by diseases."[91]

CURE has raised around $9 million to pay for more than seventy-five research projects. It has a goal of eliminating the side effects people experience as a result of taking antiseizure medication as well as getting rid of seizures. It is especially interested in preventing epilepsy, stopping it from occurring in people with brain injuries, and reversing the cognitive impact frequent seizures can have on the brain. Other research supported by CURE looks at ways of minimizing the risk of sudden unexplained death in epilepsy (SUDEP).

With funding from CURE, researchers have investigated new treatments for seizures caused by brain injury, ways to prevent seizures after a brain injury, and how heart problems may be linked to SUDEP. Research has also been conducted on new diet therapies for epilepsy, a link between breathing control and SUDEP, and using viral technology to impact the neurotransmitters in the brain and give people freedom from seizures. Other researchers are looking at ways to better treat newborn babies who have seizures. All over the world researchers assisted by CURE are working to find a solution to the puzzles of epilepsy and to allow people to live without seizures or side effects from antiseizure medications.

Getting the Word Out

People with epilepsy have input into finding a cure as well when they become actively involved in managing their health care, giving feedback about their treatments to their doctor, and participating in research studies. "It becomes more and

Taking Action

When her daughter began having seizures as a baby, Susan Axelrod did not foresee the impact they would have on her daughter's life. "We didn't realize that this would define her whole life, that she would have thousands of these afterward, that they would eat away at her brain," she says.

As she grew from a baby to a toddler to a preschooler, Lauren Axelrod would have as many as twenty-five seizures a day. She took many medications in an effort to subdue the seizures, but the drugs had side effects that would make her irritable, listless, dazed, or hyperactive.

When she was seventeen, doctors tried to pinpoint the source of her seizures with a surgical procedure. The cause was not found, and Susan Axelrod was so distraught that she cried for an entire day. Then she took action. She met with other parents and founded Citizens United for Research in Epilepsy, a nonprofit organization dedicated to increasing public awareness of epilepsy and raising money for its research.

When Lauren Axelrod was eighteen, a new drug, called Keppra, finally stopped her seizures. Although Lauren no longer has seizures, Susan Axelrod remains committed to helping others get their epilepsy under control. "Epilepsy is not benign and far too often is not treatable," Axelrod says. "We wanted the public to be aware of the death and destruction. We wanted the brightest minds to engage with the search for a cure."

Quoted in Melissa Fay Greene, "I Must Save My Child," *Parade*, February 15, 2009. www.parade.com/health/2009/02/susan-axelrod-CURE-epilepsy.html.

Susan Axlerod, whose daughter has epilepsy, founded the Citizens United for Research in Epilepsy (CURE), a nonprofit organization that increases public awareness of epilepsy and raises funds for research.

more evident that it won't be just the doctors, researchers, and scientists pushing the field forward," says Frances E. Jensen, a professor of neurology at Harvard Medical School. "There's an active role for parents and patients. They tell us when the drugs aren't working."[92]

As people with epilepsy and their family members discuss the disorder with others and raise awareness of the severity of the problem, they too are involved in the search for a cure. Although epilepsy impacts the lives of millions of people, the disorder often remains hidden and misunderstood. "Because most people with epilepsy are not in a constant state of seizure—they are, rather, in perpetual but quiet danger—their

Researchers today say parents can play an active role in the treatment of their children's epilepsy.

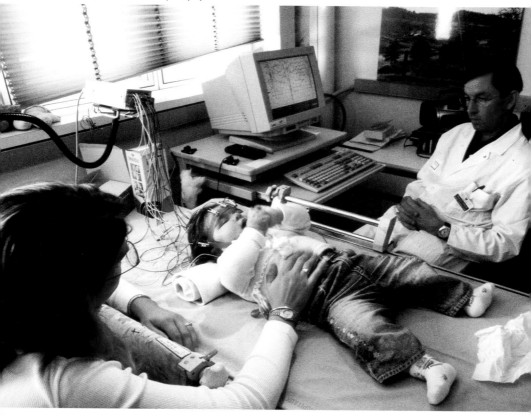

condition can appear less serious than it truly is,"[93] noted *Newsweek* editor Jon Meacham in a story on epilepsy and its impact.

To get rid of the misperceptions about epilepsy, more people will need to be educated about this brain disorder. From videos of everyday people on YouTube to comments from Hollywood celebrities on the videos on www.talkaboutit.org, more people are encouraging others to engage in discussion about epilepsy. To bring more information to students, the Epilepsy Foundation offers a program it developed with the Centers for Disease Control and Prevention called Take Charge. The five-minute video and class discussion has been shown to make a significant difference in the way people look at the condition. "We have excellent data that young people who go through this program come away with a completely different understanding," says Eric Hargis, the president and chief executive officer of the Epilepsy Foundation. "If we can get it into schools, it will take us forward light years."[94]

A Normal Life

Helping more people understand what epilepsy is and the impact it makes on people's lives can only help to raise awareness of the condition and what it means for people who live with the seizure disorder. Greater acceptance can ease the social implications of epilepsy and foster greater understanding of what it means to live with the condition every day.

Making more people aware of what it is like to have epilepsy also raises awareness of the importance of getting seizures under control. A normal life can be lived once seizures are in check, giving people with epilepsy the freedom to pursue their dreams and ambitions. American ice hockey player Chanda Gunn, who has epilepsy, won a bronze medal at the 2006 Winter Olympics. DJ Hapa, the executive director of the Scratch DJ Academy in Los Angeles, also has epilepsy. Tony Coelho became a congressman and later the chairman of the Epilepsy Foundation board. "It's certainly a serious medical condition, no doubt about it, but most people live normal lives once their seizures are controlled,"[95] Singh says.

First Aid for Seizures

It can be frightening to see a person having a seizure and natural to want to help him or her. Although nothing can be done to stop a seizure, you can do your best to make sure the person having the seizure is not injured.

While the person is having a seizure, make sure there is nothing within the person's reach that might be harmful if he or she were to hit it. Make the person as comfortable as possible. If the seizure occurs in a public place, keep gawkers away. Call 911 if the seizure lasts for more than 5 minutes. Most seizures last 1.5 to 2 minutes.

Do not try to restrain the person who is having the seizure or put anything in his or her mouth. Some people worry that a person having a seizure will swallow his or her tongue, but this is not possible. He or she should not have water, pills, or food until fully alert.

After the seizure, there is a very small chance that the person will vomit. Place the person on his or her left side, with the head turned so any vomit would come out of the mouth and reduce the person's chance of choking.

The person may be confused after the seizure. It may take five to twenty minutes for him or her to recover. Stay with the person and offer support.

A young girl receives first aid after an epileptic seizure.

To give more people with epilepsy the opportunity to live a life free from seizures and medication side effects, research is being done into treatment improvements and the search for a cure goes on. "There is cause for hope," writer Jon Meacham notes in an article in *Newsweek* that calls for more work toward an epilepsy cure. "Science is unraveling more and more of the mysteries of the brain, and perhaps the source of the cataclysmic electrical storms of epilepsy will yield its secrets."[96]

Eric Hargis of the Epilepsy Foundation is optimistic about finding effective seizure control. New medications, surgery, deep brain stimulation, and other treatment possibilities offer hope. "We're constantly seeing dramatic improvements. A number of years ago some called a diagnosis of epilepsy d-squared—diagnose and dismiss—because not a lot could be done for it," Hargis says. "It's a very promising time in terms of options."[97]

Notes

Introduction: Brain Storm

1. Sanjay Singh, telephone interview with author, May 13, 2009.
2. Eric Hargis, telephone interview with author, May 26, 2009.

Chapter One: Epilepsy and Seizures

3. Steven Schachter, "History of Epilepsy," *Epilepsy.com*. www.epilepsy.com/EPILEPSY/HISTORY.
4. Roy Sucholeiki, telephone interview with author, May 11, 2009.
5. Sucholeiki, interview.
6. Sucholeiki, interview.
7. Jerry Adler and Eliza Gray, "In the Grip of the Unknown," *Newsweek*, April 20, 2009, p. 44.
8. Steven Schachter, "What Causes Epilepsy?" *Epilepsy.com*. www.epilepsy.com/101/EP101_CAUSE.
9. Steven Schachter, "How Serious Are Seizures?" *Epilepsy .com*. www.epilepsy.com/101/ep101_death.
10. Sucholeiki, interview.
11. Sucholeiki, interview.
12. Hargis, interview.
13. Tony Coelho, "Epilepsy Gave Me a Mission," *Exceptional Parent*, March 1995. http://findarticles.com/p/aricles/mi_.
14. Hargis, interview.

Chapter Two: Seizures and Their Causes

15. Sucholeiki, interview.
16. Steven Schachter, "What Are the Risk Factors?" *Epilepsy .com*. www .epilepsy.com/101/ep101_risks.
17. Sucholeiki, interview.
18. Singh, interview.
19. Orrin Devinsky, "Myoclonic Seizures," *Epilepsy.com*. www .epilepsy.com/EPILEPSY/seizure_myoclonic.

20. Donald Weaver, *Epilepsy and Seizures: Everything You Need to Know.* Buffalo, NY: Firefly, 2001, p. 33.
21. Singh, interview.
22. Orrin Devinsky, "Complex Partial Seizures," *Epilepsy.com.* www.epilepsy.com/EPILEPSY/seizure_complexpartial.
23. Sucholeiki, interview.

Chapter Three: Living with Epilepsy
24. Mary Woodward, telephone interview with author, May 15, 2009.
25. Woodward, interview.
26. Woodward, interview.
27. Woodward, interview.
28. Woodward, interview.
29. Woodward, interview.
30. B.J. Hamrick, telephone interview with author, May 11, 2009.
31. Hamrick, interview.
32. Hamrick, interview.
33. Hamrick, interview.
34. Hamrick, interview.
35. Hamrick, interview.
36. Hamrick, interview.
37. Hamrick, interview.
38. Hamrick, interview.
39. Alex Cooper, telephone interview with author, May 12, 2009.
40. Cooper, interview.
41. Cooper, interview.
42. Cooper, interview.
43. Cooper, interview.
44. Cooper, interview.
45. Cooper, interview.
46. Heather Good, telephone interview with author, May 12, 2009.
47. Good, interview.
48. Good, interview.
49. Good, interview.

50. Good, interview.
51. Good, interview.
52. Good, interview.
53. Noel Johnson, telephone interview with author, May 22, 2009.
54. Johnson, interview.
55. Johnson, interview.
56. Johnson, interview.
57. Johnson, interview.
58. Johnson, interview.
59. Johnson, interview.
60. Johnson, interview.
61. Johnson, interview.

Chapter Four: Tests and Treatments for Epilepsy

62. Singh, interview.
63. Singh, interview.
64. Singh, interview.
65. Steven Schachter, "Will I Always Have Epilepsy?" *Epilepsy .com.* www.epilepsy.com/101/EP101_duration.
66. Sucholeiki, interview.
67. Sucholeiki, interview.
68. Singh, interview.
69. Quoted in Adler and Gray, "In the Grip of the Unknown," p. 44.
70. Quoted in Adler and Gray, "In the Grip of the Unknown," p. 44.
71. Singh, interview.
72. Singh, interview.
73. Howard L. Weiner, "Brain Mapping," *Epilepsy.com.* www .epilepsy.com/EPILEPSY/SURGERY_BRAINMAP.
74. Howard L. Weiner, "Expectations and Consequences," *Epilepsy.com.* www.epilepsy.com/EPILEPSY/surgery_ex pectations.
75. Sucholeiki, interview.
76. James Sandsted, telephone interview with author, May 24, 2009.

77. Marilyn Brownson, telephone interview with author, May 24, 2009.
78. Singh, interview.
79. Sucholeiki, interview.
80. Singh, interview.

Chapter Five: The Future of Epilepsy

81. William Davis Gaillard, telephone interview with author, June 12, 2009.
82. Quoted in Epilepsy Foundation, "Epilepsy Phenome/ Genome Project." www.epilepsyfoundation.org/research/ epgp.cfm.
83. Gaillard, interview.
84. Quoted in David Wahlberg, "University of Wisconsin–Madison Researchers Study New Drug for Epilepsy," *Wisconsin State Journal*, February 14, 2009, p. NA.
85. Howard L. Weiner, "Deep Brain Stimulation," *Epilepsy .com.* www.epilepsy.com/epilepsy/deepbrain_stimulation.
86. Singh, interview.
87. Gaillard, interview.
88. Singh, interview.
89. Singh, interview.
90. Susan Axelrod, "Agony, Hope, and Resolve," *Newsweek*, April 20, 2009, p. 49.
91. Quoted in Jon Meacham, "A Storm in the Brain," *Newsweek*, April 20, 2009, p. 41.
92. Quoted in Melissa Fay Greene, "I Must Save My Child," *Parade*, February 15, 2009. www.parade.com/health/2009/ 02/susan-axelrod-CURE-epilepsy.html.
93. Meacham, "A Storm in the Brain," p. 40.
94. Hargis, interview.
95. Singh, interview.
96. Meacham, "A Storm in the Brain," p. 40.
97. Hargis, interview.

Glossary

absence seizure: A seizure involving a brief loss of awareness, usually characterized by staring. It typically lasts less than twenty seconds and can involve blinking and brief movements of the mouth or hands.

atonic seizure: A seizure involving loss of muscle tone. The head may drop suddenly and a person may fall or drop an object that is being held.

aura: A warning that tells a person a seizure is going to occur.

clonic seizure: A seizure that impacts muscles on both sides of the body and involves jerking movements.

electroencephalograph (EEG): A test used in diagnosing epilepsy that uses a machine to record the brain's electrical activity.

epilepsy: A disorder involving recurring seizures. The seizures are caused by an abnormal electrical activity in the brain and result in an involuntary change in the way a person moves, behaves, or senses things around him or her.

ketogenic diet: A diet high in fat and low in carbohydrates. It has been successful in controlling seizures in some children.

magnetic resonance imaging (MRI): A scanning technique that uses a strong magnet to produce pictures of the brain.

magnetoencephalograph (MEG): A technique that uses the brain's magnetic activity to produce an image of the brain.

seizure: A change in behavior caused by excess electrical activity in the brain.

simple partial seizure: A seizure involving only one part of the brain.

tonic seizure: A type of seizure that involves stiffening of the muscles on both sides of the body. A person usually remains conscious during the seizure.

tonic-clonic seizure: A seizure involving stiffening of muscles, falling, and jerking. A person loses consciousness during the seizure.

vagus nerve stimulation: A device implanted in the chest that stimulates a nerve in the neck to reduce seizures.

Organizations to Contact

American Epilepsy Society
342 N. Main St.
West Hartford, CT 06117-2507
phone: (860) 586-7505
fax: (860) 586-7550
Web site: www.aesnet.org

This organization for neurological professionals promotes the exchange of information about epilepsy. It offers information about epilepsy research and grants and, through its Web site, helps patients find a doctor. It has an online journal for professionals, *Epilepsy Currents*, as well as an online database of information from its annual meetings.

Citizens United for Research in Epilepsy
730 N. Franklin St., Ste. 404
Chicago, IL 60654
phone: (312) 255-1801
fax: (312) 255-1809
Web site: www.cureepilepsy.org

This volunteer-based, nonprofit organization was founded by parents of children with epilepsy who are focused on finding a cure. It produces newsletters several times a year, and its Web site provides links to other epilepsy resources and articles about epilepsy.

Epilepsy Foundation
8301 Professional Pl.
Landover, MD 20785
phone: (800) 332-1000
Web site: www.epilepsyfoundation.org

This national voluntary agency promotes research for a cure for epilepsy. It offers programs throughout the United States as it works to improve the way people with epilepsy are perceived and ensures that people with seizures can participate in life experiences. It produces pamphlets about epilepsy for health care professionals and people with epilepsy. Its Web site also contains a list of books and other media about epilepsy.

Epilepsy Therapy Project
PO Box 742
Middleburg, VA 20118
phone: (540) 687-8077
fax: (540) 687-8066
e-mail: info@epilepsy.therapyproject.org.
Web site: www.epilepsy.com

Founded by Warren Lammert, Orrin Devinsky, and others, this organization supports research and new therapy projects related to epilepsy. It provides both basic and detailed information about epilepsy through its Web site, epilepsy.com. The site contains a list of books about epilepsy, living with epilepsy, and epilepsy treatment. It also contains a list of books for children, teens, and families.

Finding a Cure for Epilepsy and Seizures (FACES)
NYU Langone Medical Center
530 First Ave.
New York, NY 10016
phone: (212) 263-7300
Web site: www.med.nyu.edu/cec/programs/faces.html

FACES is the nonprofit arm of the New York University Comprehensive Epilepsy Center. Its mission is to improve the quality of life for people with epilepsy through research into new treatments, education, and awareness initiatives. Its Web site contains information about its latest research and links to research articles.

International League Against Epilepsy
Avenue Jules Bordetlaan 142
B-1140 Evere

Brussels, Belgium
phone: +32 (0) 2 761 1647
fax: +32 (0) 2 761 1699
Web site: www.ilae-epilepsy.org

Founded in 1909, this organization spreads information about epilepsy and promotes research, education, and training. It also aims to improve services to those with epilepsy and care for patients through prevention, diagnosis, and treatment. It produces brochures in English, Russian, Spanish, and German about epilepsy treatment, first aid, diagnosis, and other issues as well as a biannual newsletter. Its official journal, *Epilepsia*, provides current clinical and research results. Other journals it produces include *Epilepsy & Behavior*, with information on behavioral aspects of seizures and epilepsy; *Epilepsy Research*, which looks at fresh approaches to the study of epilepsy and epilepsy treatment; *Seizure*, which looks at issues relating to epilepsy and seizure disorders; *Epileptic Disorders*, which focuses on the clinical aspect of epilepsy and related disorders; and *Epilepsies*, which is published in French and covers advances in epilepsy.

For Further Reading

Books

Carl W. Bazil, *Living Well with Epilepsy and Other Seizure Disorders: An Expert Explains What You Really Need to Know.* New York: HarperCollins, 2004. This book offers treatment options, support, and answers for people living with epilepsy.

Ruth Bjorklund, *Epilepsy.* Tarrytown, NY: Marshall Cavendish Benchmark, 2007. A book for children that offers easy-to-understand information about epilepsy.

Orrin Devinsky, *Epilepsy: Patient and Family Guide.* New York: Demos Medical, 2007. Written by a leading expert in epilepsy, this guide for patients offers insightful information and answers common questions about the disorder.

Periodicals

Jerry Adler and Eliza Gray, "In the Grip of the Unknown," *Newsweek,* April 20, 2009. This article looks at people impacted by epilepsy and talks about what is being done to find a cure. It highlights the work of Orrin Devinsky at New York University, points out the seriousness of the disorder, and looks at what is being done to find a cure.

Melissa Fay Greene, "I Must Save My Child," *Parade,* February 15, 2009. www.parade.com/heatlh/2009/02/susan-axelrod-CURE-epilepsy.html. Susan Axelrod talks about the impact that her daughter Lauren's epilepsy has had on her family and how it inspired her to found an organization dedicated to finding a cure.

Jon Meacham, "A Storm in the Brain," *Newsweek,* April 20, 2009. This article provides an overview of the impact of epilepsy and an explanation of what happens during a seizure.

Web Sites

American Epilepsy Outreach Foundation (www.epilepsy outreach.org). This site provides information about epilepsy diagnosis, treatment, and syndromes as well as news updates relating to epilepsy.

American Epilepsy Society (www.aesnet.org). The society's Web site provides news about epilepsy and highlights educational opportunities. It helps patients find a doctor and offers professional development information.

Centers for Disease Control and Prevention (www.cdc .gov). This site offers information on many health issues. Search for *epilepsy* to find a definition of the disorder, basic information, statistics, and resources.

Citizens United for Research in Epilepsy (www.cure epilepsy.org). This Web site includes information about epilepsy and people who are dealing with the disorder. It also highlights research projects being undertaken to find a cure for epilepsy.

Epilepsy Foundation (www.epilepsyfoundation.org). This site provides information about epilepsy and offers networking options for people who are living with epilepsy to find answers to their questions. It also offers opportunities to network with people who are living with epilepsy.

Epilepsy.com (www.epilepsy.com). This Web site, supported by the Epilepsy Therapy Project, has in-depth information from epilepsy professionals. It offers well-written, easily understandable basic information about the disorder as well as in-depth information for professionals. The site also includes interactive features, allowing people with epilepsy to participate in forums and have questions answered.

International League Against Epilepsy (www.ilae-epilepsy.org). This site offers information about the worldwide organization and its chapters.

National Institute of Neurological Disorders and Stroke (www.ninds.nih.gov). The institute offers information on a number of disorders impacting the brain, including epilepsy.

Talk About It! (www.talkaboutit.org). Through video, this site explains what epilepsy is and offers support for those with epilepsy.

Index

Picture Credits

Cover photo: © Richard T. Nowitz/Encyclopedia/Corbis
AP Images, 54-55, 59
Bob Larson/MCT/Landov, 73
BSIP/Photo Researchers, Inc., 15, 32, 39
Cosmocyte/Photo Researchers, Inc., 18-19
Dr. Jurgen Scriba/Photo Researchers, Inc., 64
Gil Cohen Magen/Reuters/Landov, 81
Joe McNally/Getty Images, 41, 69
John Bavosi/Photo Researchers, Inc., 9
Josh Sher/Photo Researchers, Inc., 67
Klaus Rose/dpa/Landov, 61
Mark Clarke/Photo Researchers, Inc., 35
Medical-On-Line/Alamy, 76
Medical Body Scans/Photo Researchers, Inc., 79
National Library of Medicine/Photo Researchers, Inc., 23
Pedro Ugarte/AFP/Getty Images, 12, 86
PHANIE/Photo Researchers, Inc., 20, 45, 84
Phil Velasquez/MCT/Landov, 83
Richard T. Nowitz/Phototake, Inc./Alamy, 50
Richard T. Nowitz/Photo Researchers, Inc., 29
Simon Fraser/Photo Researchers, Inc., 27
STR/Reuters/Landov, 53
Tim Boyle/Getty Images, 42

About the Author

Terri Dougherty lives in Appleton, Wisconsin, where she writes, edits, and enjoys life with her husband, three children (Kyle, Rachel, and Emily), and two cats. She has written more than seventy books for children and enjoys learning something new with each title.